THE
AUTOBIOGRAPHY
OF
GEORGE
MULLER

YOU TOO CAN EXPERIENCE
MIRACULOUS ANSWERS TO PRAYER!

WHITAKER HOUSE

Publisher's note:
This new edition from Whitaker House has been updated
for the modern reader. Words, expressions, and sentence
structure have been revised for clarity and readability.

Scripture quotations are taken from the King James
Version (KJV) of the Holy Bible.

THE AUTOBIOGRAPHY OF GEORGE MÜLLER
mass market edition

ISBN-13: 978-0-88368-159-6
ISBN-10: 0-88368-159-5
Printed in the United States of America
© 1985 by Whitaker House

Whitaker House
1030 Hunt Valley Circle
New Kensington, PA 15068
www.whitakerhouse.com

14 15 16 17 18 19 20 **ᴌᴌ** 12 11 10 09 08 07 06

THE AUTOBIOGRAPHY OF GEORGE MULLER

CONTENTS

INTRODUCTION

What is meant by the prayer of faith? What is the significance of the passages in the Old and New Testaments which refer to it? Were these promises limited to Bible times or have they been left to us as a legacy until Jesus returns?

These questions attract a great deal of attention among believers. The thoughtful Christian who reads any of the wonderful promises in Scripture often pauses to ask himself, "What can these words mean? Can it be that God has made these promises to me? Do I really have permission to commit all my little concerns to a God of infinite wisdom, believing that He will take charge of them and direct them according to His boundless love and absolute omniscience? Is prayer really a transcendent power which accomplishes what no other power can, overruling all other agencies and rendering them subservient to its own wonderful effectiveness? If this is true, then why shouldn't I always draw near to God in full confidence that He will do as He has said?''

A most remarkable instance of the effectiveness of prayer is recorded in this book. A young German Christian named George Muller answered a call from the Lord to help the poor children of Bristol in England. He preached the gospel to a small company of believers from whom, at his own suggestion, he received no salary. His only support was the voluntary offerings of his brethren. In answer to prayer, funds were received as needed.

After a few years, God called him to establish a house for the care and education of orphans. He was drawn to this work, not only from motives of benevolence, but from a desire to convince men that God does answer prayer.

Mr. Muller began this work in such a manner that aid could not be expected from anyone but God. He did not, of course, expect God to create gold and silver and put them into his hands. He knew that God could incline the hearts of men to aid him, and he believed that if the work was of Him, He would meet every need. Thus, in child-like simplicity, he looked to God, and all that he needed was furnished as punctually as if he were a millionaire drawing regularly on his bank account.

George Muller was a slender man, standing six feet tall in his boots. His dark brown eyes twinkled with a benevolent expression as he talked. He dressed in black, except for a white necktie fastened with a plain pin in front. His jet black hair was coarse and carefully combed in place. Whether in the pulpit or on the street, his entire appearance was a perfect model of neatness and order.

He mastered six languages—Latin, Greek, Hebrew, German, French, and English. He read and understood Dutch and two or three Oriental languages. His library consisted of a Hebrew Bible, three Greek Testaments, a Greek concordance and lexicon, with a half dozen different versions of the Bible and copies of the best translations in several languages. These constituted his *entire library!*

When he preached, he would read a whole chapter or part of one and then proceed to draw out rich treasures that made it worth crossing the ocean to hear. His method of preaching caused the members of his congregation to become mighty in the Scriptures. They were better qualified to guide inquiring souls to Christ than many young ministers who had spent three years in a theological seminary.

Most men would consider such an extensive ministry as his to be a reasonable excuse for cutting short their prayer and study time. Not so with Mr. Muller. In his prayer closet, alone with God and the Bible, he would gird up the loins of his mind and burnish his armor for the battles of the day. With absolute confidence and childlike simplicity, he believed every Word that God had spoken. He eagerly returned to God's Word several times each day as though he was in constant communication with heaven, receiving fresh letters of instruction and precious promises from his heavenly Father.

Muller never studied the Bible for others. He studied only for himself to find out what His Father required of him. He became so impregnated with God's truth that, when he spoke of God, his listeners would be reminded of the words of our Savior in John 7:38, for from him seemed to flow "rivers of living water."

His prayers were offered in simple language with a humble and fervent spirit. Because he knew his Father was so rich, benevolent, and forgiving, he was free to ask for and obtain great blessings. But the most remarkable feature about his prayer was that he asked for everything in the name of the Lord Jesus Christ. To glorify Christ and magnify His name above every name seemed to be the all-pervading theme that filled his heart and life.

The amount of labor Mr. Muller performed is amazing to us today. The almost endless variety would be more than most other men could bear. Yet, he was always calm, peaceful, and in a prayerful frame of mind, casting all his cares upon the Lord.

It was George Muller's greatest hope that his record of God's faithfulness to him would encourage believers to develop faith like his own—the faith without which it is impossible to please God; the faith that works by love and purifies the heart; the faith that removes mountains of obstacles out of our path; the faith that takes hold of God's strength and is the substance of things hoped for and the evidence of things not seen. May this faith fill the hearts and lives of those who read this book.

●

Chapter 1

AN UNLIKELY PREACHER

I was born at Kroppenstaedt in the kingdom of Prussia on September 27, 1805. My father, a tax collector, educated his children on worldly principles, and my brother and I slipped easily into many sins. Before I was ten years old, I had repeatedly stolen government money which was entrusted to my father and forced him to make up the losses.

When I was eleven years old, my father sent me to Halberstadt to be prepared to study at the university. He wanted me to become a clergyman—not that I would serve God, but that I would have a comfortable life. Studying, reading novels, and indulging in sinful practices were my favorite pastimes.

My mother died suddenly when I was fourteen years old. That night I played cards until two in the morning, and went to a tavern the next day. Her death made no lasting impression on me. Instead, I grew worse.

Three days before my confirmation and communion, I was guilty of gross immorality. The day before my confirmation, I lied to the clergyman rather than confess my sins. In this state of heart, without prayer, true repentance, faith, or knowledge of the plan of salvation, I was confirmed and took part in the Lord's Supper. Because I had some feeling about the solemnity of the occasion, I stayed home during the afternoon and evening.

That summer I spent some time studying but more in playing the piano and guitar, reading novels, frequenting taverns, making resolutions to become different, and breaking them almost as fast as I made them. I was glad when my father obtained an appointment for me at a school near Magdeburg because I thought that if I left my sinful companions, I would live a different life. But I grew still more idle and continued to live in all sorts of sin.

In November I went on a pleasure trip where I spent six days in sin. My father discovered my absence before I returned, so I took all the money I could find and went to Brunswick. After spending a week at Brunswick in an expensive hotel, my money was gone. I then went, without money, to another hotel for a week. At last, the owner of the hotel, suspecting that I had no money, asked for payment and took my best clothes as security.

I walked about six miles to an inn and began to live as if I had plenty of money. On the third morning, I went quietly out of the yard and ran off.

By this time the innkeeper became suspicious and had me arrested. The police questioned me for about three hours and sent me to jail. At the age of sixteen I became an inmate of a prison, dwelling with thieves and murderers.

After a year, the commissioner who had tried my case told my father of my conduct. I was kept in prison until he sent the money for my traveling expenses, my debt to the inn, and my stay in prison. My father arrived two days later, beat me severely, and took me home to Schoenebeck. Through more lying and persuading, I convinced him to allow me to enter school at Nordhausen the following autumn.

I lived in the house of the principal at Nordhausen. Through my conduct, I grew highly in his favor. He had such a high esteem for me that I was held up by him as an example to the rest of the class. But while I was outwardly gaining the esteem of my fellow men, I did not care in the least about God. As a result of my sinful lifestyle, I became ill and was confined to my room for thirteen weeks.

During my illness, I felt no real remorse and cared nothing about the Word of God. I owned more than three hundred books, but no Bible. Now and then I wanted to become a different person and tried to amend my conduct, particularly when I went to the Lord's Supper. The day before attending a communion service, I used to abstain from certain things. On the day itself, I promised

God that I would become a better person, thinking that somehow God would induce me to reform. But after one or two days, I forgot everything and was as bad as before.

At age 20 I received honorable recommendations and became a member of the University of Halle. I even obtained permission to preach in the Lutheran church. But I felt as truly unhappy and far from God as ever.

I now resolved to change my lifestyle for two reasons: first, because unless I reformed, no parish would choose me as their pastor; and secondly, without a considerable knowledge of theology, I would never earn a good living. But the moment I entered Halle, all my resolutions disappeared. I resumed my loose living even though I was in the seminary. Deep in my heart, I longed to renounce this wretched life. I did not enjoy it, and I had sense enough to see that one day it would ruin me completely. Still, I felt no sorrow about offending God.

One day while in a tavern with some of my wild friends, I saw one of my former classmates named Beta. I met him four years earlier at Halberstadt; and, because he was so quiet and serious, I despised him. It now appeared wise for me to choose him as my friend, thinking that better companions would help me improve my conduct.

The Spirit of God was working in Beta's heart at Halberstadt, but Beta was a backslider. He tried to put off the ways of God and enjoy the world he had known little about before. *I* sought his friendship because I thought it would lead me to a moral life, and *he* gladly became my friend because he thought it would bring him some good times.

In August, Beta, myself, and two other students drove through the country for four days. When we returned, my love for traveling was stronger than ever, and I suggested that we set off for Switzerland. Through forged letters from our parents, we procured passports and acquired as much money as we could. We left school and traveled for forty-three days.

I had now obtained the desire of my heart—I had seen Switzerland. But I was still far from being happy. On this journey I acted like Judas. I managed the money so that the journey cost me only two thirds of what it cost my friends. By many lies, I satisfied my father's questions concerning the expenses.

During my three weeks of summer vacation, I resolved to live differently in the future, and I was different—for a few days. But when vacation was over, and new students came with fresh money, all my resolutions were soon forgotten. I easily slipped back into my old habits. Nevertheless, the God whom I dishonored by my wicked behavior and unrepentant spirit had not given up on me.

Chapter 2

THE PRODIGAL'S RETURN

Despite my sinful lifestyle and cold heart, God had mercy on me. I was as careless about Him as ever. I had no Bible and had not read any Scripture for years. I seldom went to church; and, out of custom only, I took the Lord's Supper twice a year. I never heard the gospel preached. Nobody told me that Jesus meant for Christians, by the help of God, to live according to the Holy Scriptures. In short, I did not have the least idea that there were people who were different from myself.

One Saturday afternoon in November, I took a walk with my friend Beta. He told me that he had begun to visit a Christian's home every Saturday where there was a prayer meeting. He said that they read the Bible, sang, prayed, and read a printed sermon.

When I heard this, I felt as if I had found the treasure I had been seeking all my life. We went to the meeting together that evening. I did not understand the joy that believers have in seeing any sinner become interested in the things of God, so I apologized for coming. I will never forget the kind answer of the dear brother. He said, "Come as often as you please. Our house and hearts are open to you."

We sat down and sang a hymn. Then brother Kayser, now a missionary in Africa, knelt and asked a blessing on our meeting. His kneeling down made a deep impression on me, for I had never seen anyone on his knees before, nor had I ever prayed on my knees. He read a chapter from the Bible and a printed sermon. At the end of the meeting, we sang another hymn, and then the owner of the house prayed. While he prayed, I thought, "I could not pray as well, although I have more education than this man."

The entire evening made a deep impression on me. I felt happy, although if I had been asked why, I could not have clearly explained it. When we walked home, I said to Beta, "Everything we have seen on our journey to Switzerland and all of our former pleasures are nothing in comparison with this evening."

The Lord begins His work in different ways with different people. I have no doubt that on that evening, He began a work of grace in me. Even though I scarcely had any knowledge of who God truly was, that evening was the turning point in my life.

For the next several days, I went regularly to this brother's house, and we read the Scriptures together. The Lord and the Word were so exciting to me that I could not wait until Saturday came again. Now my life became very different, although I did not give up every sin at once. I did give up my wicked companions, going to taverns, and habitual lying. I read the Scriptures, prayed often, loved the brethren, went to church with the right motives, and openly professed Christ although my fellow students laughed at me.

As I read missionary newsletters, I was inspired to become a missionary myself. I prayed frequently concerning this matter for several weeks. A few months later, I met a devoted young brother named Hermann Ball, a learned and wealthy man. He chose to labor in Poland among the Jews as a missionary rather than live a comfortable life near his family. His example made a deep impression on me. For the first time in my life, I was able to give myself up to the Lord fully and without reservation.

The peace of God which passes all understanding now filled my life. I wrote to my father and brother, encouraging them to seek the Lord and telling them how happy I was. I believed that if they saw the way to happiness, they would gladly embrace it. To my great surprise, they replied with an angry letter.

The Lord sent Dr. Tholuck, a professor of divinity, to Halle. As a result, a few believing students transferred to Halle from other universities. As I became acquainted with other Christians, the Lord helped me to grow in Him.

My former desire to give myself to missionary service returned, and I went to my father to ask his permission. Without it, I would not be admitted to any of the German missionary institutions. My father was greatly displeased and severely reproached me, saying that he had spent so much money on my education hoping that he could comfortably spend his last days with me in a parsonage. Now, all these prospects had come to nothing. He told me that he would no longer consider me his son. Then he wept and begged me to change my mind.

The Lord helped me to bear this difficult trial. Although I needed more money than ever before, I decided never to take any more from my father. I still had two more years of seminary left. It seemed wrong to let my father support me when he had no guarantee that I would become what he wanted me to be—a clergyman earning a good living.

The Lord enabled me to keep this resolution. Several American gentlemen, three of whom were professors in American colleges, came to Halle for literary research. Because they did not understand German, Dr. Tholuck recommended me to teach them. Some of these gentlemen were Christians, and they paid so well for the instruction I gave them and for the lectures I wrote for them that I had enough money for school and some to spare.

The Lord richly made up to me the little I had given up for His sake.

Although I was still very weak and ignorant in faith, I longed to win souls for Christ. Every month I circulated about three hundred missionary papers, distributed many tracts, and wrote letters to some of my former companions in sin.

A local schoolmaster held a morning prayer meeting a few miles away, and I decided to attend. At that time, however, I did not know that he was not a believer. He later told me that he had held the prayer meetings merely out of kindness to a relative. The sermons he read were not his own, but copied out of a book. He also told me that he had been impressed with my kindness and that I had been instrumental in leading him to care about the things of God. Ever since that time, I knew him as a true brother in the Lord.

This schoolmaster asked me to preach in his parish because the aged clergyman needed my assistance. I thought that by learning a sermon written by a spiritual man I might minister to the people; so I put the sermon into a suitable form and memorized it.

I got through the morning service, but I did not enjoy preaching. I decided to preach the gospel in the afternoon and began by reading the fifth chapter of Matthew. Immediately as I began to teach on, "Blessed are the poor in spirit," I felt the annointing of the Holy Spirit. My morning sermon had been too complicated for the people to understand, but now they listened to me with great interest. My own peace and joy were great, and I felt this was a blessed work.

On my return trip to Halle, I thought, "This is the way I would always like to preach." But then I thought that while this type of preaching might work for illiterate country people, it would never be accepted at the well-educated assembly in town. I knew that the truth should be preached at all costs, but I thought it should be presented in a different form, suited to the hearers. I remained unsettled about choosing a style of preaching for some time. Because I did not yet understand the work of the Spirit, I did not realize the powerlessness of human eloquence.

Although I regularly went to church when I did not preach myself, I seldom heard the truth because there was no enlightened clergyman in the town. When Dr. Tholuck or any other godly minister preached, I often walked ten or fifteen miles to enjoy the privilege of hearing the Word.

In addition to the Saturday evening meeting, I fed my faith at a meeting every Sunday evening with six other believing students. Before I left the university, the number increased to twenty. In these meetings, one or more of the brethren prayed, we read Scriptures, sang hymns, someone exhorted the group, and we read some edifying writings of godly men. I opened my heart to the brethren for prayer and encouragement to keep me from backsliding.

I was growing in the faith and knowledge of Jesus, but I still preferred reading religious books instead of the Scriptures. I read tracts, missionary newsletters, sermons, and biographies of Christian people. God is the author of the Bible, and only the truth it contains will lead people to true happiness. A Christian should read this precious Book every day with earnest prayer and meditation. But like many believers, I preferred to read the works of uninspired men rather than the oracles of the living God. Consequently, I remained a spiritual baby both in knowledge and grace.

The last and most important means of growing in the Lord, prayer, was also something I greatly neglected. I prayed often and generally with sincerity. But if I had prayed more earnestly, I would have made much more rapid progress in my faith. Despite my slowness to grasp spiritual principles, however, God showed His great patience toward me and helped me to grow steadily in Him.

Chapter 3

STEPPING OUT INTO MINISTRY

Dr. Tholuck informed me that the Continental Society in England intended to send a minister to Bucharest to help an aged brother in the work of the Lord. After consideration and prayer, I offered my services. Despite all my weaknesses, I had a great desire to live wholly for God. Unexpectedly, my father gave his consent, although Bucharest was over a thousand miles away.

I now prepared for the work of the Lord with diligence and pondered the sufferings which might await me. I had once fully served Satan; but now, drawn by the love of Christ, I was willing to suffer affliction for the sake of Jesus. Earnestly, I prayed about my future work.

At the end of October, Hermann Ball, the missionary to the Polish Jews, said that his health would soon force him to give up his work. When I heard this, I felt a strong desire to take his place. The Hebrew language suddenly became exciting to me even though I had previously studied it only from a sense of duty. Now I studied for many weeks with eagerness and delight.

While I still desired to take brother Ball's place and delighted in learning Hebrew, I called on Dr. Tholuck. Unaware of my thoughts, he suddenly asked me whether I had ever had a desire to be a missionary to the Jews. He was an agent with the London Missionary Society for promoting Christianity among them. I was astonished by his question and told him what had been on my mind for the last several weeks. I added that it was not proper for me to consider any other service because I had already agreed to go to Bucharest. He agreed.

When I came home, however, our conversation burned like fire within me. The next morning, all my desire for going to Bucharest was gone. This seemed to be very wrong and fleshly of me, and I entreated the Lord to restore my former desire to labor there. He graciously did so almost immediately. Meanwhile, my earnestness in studying Hebrew and my love for it continued.

About ten days later, Dr. Tholuck received a letter from the Continental Society. Because of the war between the Turks and the Russians, they had decided not to send a minister to Bucharest since it was the center of war. Dr. Tholuck asked me again what I thought about becoming a missionary to the Jews. After prayer and consulting with spiritually mature brethren, I concluded that I should offer myself to the society, leaving my future with the Lord.

Dr. Tholuck wrote to the society in London and received an answer in a few weeks. They had a number of questions for me and my acceptance depended on my satisfactory answers. After replying to this first communication, I received a letter from London. The committee decided to take me as a missionary student for six months probation, provided I would come to London.

One obstacle stood in the way of my leaving the country. Every Prussian male was obligated to serve three years as a soldier, but those who finished their studies at the university only had to serve one year. I could not obtain a passport out of the country until I had either served my time or been exempted by the king himself. I hoped the latter would be the case. It was a well-known fact that those who had given themselves to missionary service had always been exempted. Certain influential Christian brothers who were living in the capital wrote to the king. He replied that the matter must be referred to the government officials, and no exception was made in my favor.

My chief concern now was how I could be exempted from military duty and obtain a passport for England. But the more I tried, the greater the difficulty appeared to be. By the middle of January, it seemed as if my only recourse was to become a soldier.

One more avenue remained untried—it was my

last resort. A major in the army was a Christian and on good terms with one of the chief generals. He proposed that I start the process of entering the army. Since I was still very weak physically from a former illness, I would be found unfit for military service.

I believe that the Lord had allowed things to happen this way to show me that my friends would be unable to obtain a passport for me until He was ready. But now the time had come. The King of kings intended that I go to England because He would make me a blessing there despite my unworthiness. At a time when hope had almost been given up, and when the last plan had been tried, everything began to fall into place. The doctors examined me and declared that I was unfit for military service. The chief general himself signed the papers, and I got a complete dismissal for life from all military duty.

I came to England physically weakened and soon became very ill. In my estimation, I was beyond recovery. Yet the weaker I became in body, the happier I was in spirit. Every sin I had ever committed was brought to mind, but I realized that I was washed and made completely clean in the blood of Jesus. This realization brought me great peace, and I longed to die and be with Christ.

When my doctor came to see me, my prayer was, "Lord, You know that he does not know what is best for me. Therefore, please direct him." When I took my medicine, my prayer was, "Lord, You know that this medicine is no more than a little water. Now please, Lord, let it produce the effect which is for my good and for Your glory. Let me either soon be taken to heaven, or let me be restored. Lord, do with me as You think best!"

After I had been ill for two weeks, my health began to improve. Some friends asked me to go into the country for the fresh air. When I asked the doctor, he said that it was the best thing I could do. A few days later, I left for the little country town of Teignmouth.

I had a great deal of time to study the Bible while I recovered. During this time, God showed me that His Word alone is our standard of judgment in spiritual things. The Word can be explained only by the Holy Spirit who is the teacher of His people. I had not understood the work of the Holy Spirit in a practical way before that time.

Now I learned that the Father chose us before the foundation of the world. He originated the wonderful plan of our redemption, and He also arranged the way it was to be brought about. The Son fulfilled the law and bore the punishment due to our sins, satisfying the justice of God. Finally, the Holy Spirit alone can teach us about our sinful state, show us the need of a Savior, enable us to believe in Christ, explain the Scriptures to us, and help us preach the Word.

The Lord enabled me to put this last aspect of

the Holy Spirit to the test by laying aside my commentaries and almost every other book and simply reading the Word of God. That first evening when I shut myself in my room to pray and meditate over the Scriptures, I learned more in a few hours than during the last several months.

After my return to London, I decided to do something to help my brothers in the seminary. I suggested we meet together every morning from six until eight to pray and read the Scriptures. After the evening prayer, my communion with God was so sweet that I would continue praying until after midnight. Then I would go to a brother's room, and we would pray together until one or two in the morning. Even then, I was sometimes so full of joy that I could not sleep. At six in the morning, I would again call the brethren together for prayer.

After I had been in London for ten days and had been confined to the house because of my studies, my health again began to decline. I decided to stop spending the little energy I had left on my studies and go to work for the Lord. I wrote to the missionary Society and asked them to send me out at once. They sent me no reply, but continued to support me while I studied.

After waiting six weeks, and in the meantime seeking to work for the Lord, it occurred to me that I should begin to labor among the Jews in London whether I had the title of missionary or not. I distributed tracts among the Jews and invited them to come and talk to me about the things of God. I preached to them in the places where they gathered and read the Scriptures regularly with about fifty Jewish boys. I had the honor of being reproached and ill-treated for the name of Jesus. The Lord gave me grace, however, and I was never kept from the work by any danger or the prospect of suffering.

Toward the close of 1829, I began to doubt whether it was right for me to be supported by the London Society. It seemed unscriptural to me for a servant of Christ to put himself under the control and direction of anyone but the Lord. The society and I exchanged letters on this subject, and in complete kindness and love, we dissolved our relationship. I was now free to preach the gospel wherever the Lord opened the way.

In December, I stayed with some Christian friends who lived in Exmouth. The second day after my arrival, a brother said to me, "I have been praying for a month that the Lord would do something at Lympstone, a large parish where there is little spiritual light. I believe you would be allowed to preach there." Ready to speak of Jesus wherever the Lord might open a door, and desiring to be faithful to the truths which He taught me, I went. I easily obtained permission to preach twice the next Sunday.

God blessed and encouraged me as I worked for His Kingdom. I began learning to be sensitive to His Spirit. He taught me how to study and revealed more of His Word to me. More opportunities to preach were opened, and I rejoiced to serve my Lord Jesus Christ.

Chapter 4

PREACHING, STUDYING, AND GROWTH

After I had preached about three weeks in the vicinity of Exmouth, I went to Teignmouth expecting to stay there ten days to preach the Word among the brethren. One young woman came to know Jesus Christ as her Savior that first evening. This blessed me because none of the resident ministers liked the sermon. The Lord judges so differently from man!

The next week, after preaching daily in the chapel, I was asked to stay and be their minister. Because of certain opposition, I decided to stay until I was formally rejected. I preached again on the Lord's day, although many did not enjoy hearing my sermon. Some people left and never returned. Others came to the chapel who had not been in the habit of attending before I came. A spirit of inquiry and a searching of the Scriptures suddenly began. People wanted to know whether the things I said were true. Most importantly, God set His seal of approval on the work by converting sinners.

I preached at this chapel as a visiting minister for twelve weeks. During this time, without my asking, the Lord graciously supplied my worldly needs through two brothers. When the twelve weeks were over, the eighteen member church unanimously invited me to become their pastor.

I now changed my opinion about the best method of preparing for public ministry of the Word. Rather than presuming to know what is best for the hearers, I ask the Lord to graciously teach me the subject I should speak about, or the portion of His Word I should explain. Sometimes I will have a particular subject or passage on my mind before asking Him. If, after prayer, I feel persuaded that I should speak on that subject, I study it, but still leave myself open to the Lord to change it if He pleases.

Frequently, however, I have no subject in my mind before I pray. In this case, I wait on my knees for an answer, trying to listen for the voice of the Spirit to direct me. Then, if a passage of subject is brought to mind, I again ask the Lord if this is His will. Sometimes I ask repeatedly, especially if the subject or text is a difficult one. If after prayer, my mind is peaceful about it, I take this to be the text. But I still leave myself open to the Lord for direction, in case He decides to alter it, or if I have been mistaken.

Sometimes I still do not have a text after praying. At first I was puzzled by this, but I have learned to simply continue with my regular reading of the Scriptures, praying while I read for a text. I have had to read five, ten, even twenty chapters before the Lord has given me a text. Many times I have even had to go to the meeting place without a subject. But I have always obtained it, perhaps, only a few minutes before I was going to speak.

The Lord always helps me when I preach, provided I have earnestly sought Him in private. A preacher cannot know the hearts of the individuals in the congregation or what they need to hear. But the Lord knows; and if the preacher renounces his own wisdom, he will be assisted by the Lord. But if he is determined to choose a subject in his own wisdom, he should not be surprised when he sees little fruit resulting from his labors.

When I have obtained the text in the above way, whether it is a verse or a whole chapter or more, I ask the Lord to graciously teach me by His Holy Spirit while I meditate over the passages. I write down notes as the Word is opened to me to see how well I understand the passage. It is also useful to later refer to what I have written.

I seldom use any other study aids besides the Scriptures and some good translations in other languages. My chief help is prayer. Whenever I study a single part of divine truth, I always gain some light about it after praying and meditating over it. Extensive prayer is often difficult because of the weakness of the flesh, physical infirmities, and a full schedule. But no one should expect to see much good resulting from his labors if he does not spend time in prayer and meditation.

I then leave myself entirely in the hands of the Lord, asking Him to bring to mind what I have learned in my prayer closet. He faithfully does this and often teaches me more while I am preaching. The *preparation* for the public ministry of the Word is even more excellent than preaching in church. To live in constant communion with the Lord, and to be habitually and frequently in meditation over the truth is its own reward.

Expounding the Scriptures is most beneficial, especially when studying a whole gospel or epistle. This may be done either by entering minutely into the meaning of every verse or by giving the main points and leading the hearers to see the overall meaning of the whole book. Expounding the Scriptures encourages the congregation to bring their Bibles to church, and everything that leads believers to value the Scriptures is important.

This method of preaching is more beneficial to the hearers than if, on a single verse, some remarks are made so that the portion of Scripture is scarcely anything but a motto for the subject. Few people have grace to meditate for hours over the Word. Thus, exposition may open the Scriptures to them and create in them a desire to meditate for themselves. When they again read over the portion of the Word which has been expounded, they will remember what has been said. Thus, it leaves a more lasting impression on their minds.

Expounding large portions of the Word, such as an entire gospel or epistle, leads the teacher to consider portions of the Word which he might otherwise overlook. This keeps him from speaking too much on favorite subjects and leaning too much to particular parts of truth—a tendency which will surely sooner or later injure both himself and his hearers.

Simplicity in expression is of utmost importance. The teacher should speak so that even children and people who cannot read may be able to understand him, as far as the natural mind can comprehend the things of God. Every congregation has people of various educational and social backgrounds. The expounder of the truth of God speaks for God and for eternity. It is unlikely that he will benefit the hearers unless he uses plain speech.

If the preacher strives to speak according to the rules of this world, he may please many, particularly those who have a literary taste. But he is less likely to become an instrument in the hands of God for the conversion of sinners or for the building up of the saints. Neither eloquence nor depth of thought makes a truly great preacher. Only a life of prayer and meditation will render him a vessel ready for the Master's use and fit to be employed in the conversion of sinners and in the edification of the saints.

The anointing of the Holy Spirit helps me greatly when I preach. I would never attempt to teach the truth of God by my own power. One day before preaching at Teignmouth, I had more time than usual, so I prayed and meditated for six hours in preparation for the evening meeting. After I had spoken a little while, I felt that I was speaking in my own strength rather than God's power. I told the brethren that I felt as though I was not preaching under the anointing and asked them to pray. After I continued a little longer, I felt the same and therefore ended my sermon and proposed that we have a meeting for prayer. We did so, and I was particularly assisted by the Holy Spirit the next time I preached.

I am glad that I learned the importance of ministering in God's power alone. I can do all things through Christ, but without Him, I can accomplish nothing.

Chapter 5

LEARNING TO LIVE BY FAITH

On October 7, 1830, I was united in marriage to Miss Mary Groves. This step was taken after much prayer and from a full conviction that it was better for me to be married. I have never regretted either the step itself or the choice, but I am truly grateful to God for giving me such a wife.

About this time, I began to have conscientious objections against receiving a salary by renting pews. According to James 2:1-6, this practice is against the mind of the Lord because the poor brethren cannot afford as good a seat as the rich. A brother may gladly give something toward my support if the choice is up to him. But when he has other expenses, I do not know whether he pays his money grudgingly or cheerfully, and God loves a cheerful giver. The renting of pews is also a snare to the servant of Christ. Fear of offending those who pay his salary has kept many ministers from preaching the uncompromising Word of God.

For these reasons, I told the brethren that at the

end of October, 1830, I would give up my regular salary. After I had given my reasons for doing so, I read Philippians 4. If the saints wanted to give something toward my support by voluntary gifts, I had no objection to receiving it either in money or provisions. A few days later, I realized that if I personally received every single gift, much of my time and that of the donors would be lost. Also, the poor might be embarrassed to give me a small amount. Others might give more than if the gifts were anonymous. Therefore, it would still be doubtful whether the gifts were given grudgingly or cheerfully. For these reasons, we put a box in the chapel with a sign explaining that whoever had a desire to give something toward my support could put his offering into the box.

My wife and I had the grace to take the Lord's commandment in Luke 12:33 literally, "Sell that ye have, and give alms." We never regretted taking that step. God blessed us abundantly as He taught us to trust in Him alone. When we were down to our last few shillings, we told Him about our needs and depended on Him to provide. He never failed us.

On November 18, 1830, our money was reduced to about eight shillings. When I was praying with my wife in the morning, I was led to ask the Lord for money. Four hours later, a sister said to me, "Do you want any money?"

I replied, "I told the brethren when I gave up

my salary that I would tell the Lord only about my wants."

She said, "But He has told me to give you some money. About two weeks ago I asked Him what I should do for Him, and He told me to give you some money. Last Saturday the thought came again powerfully to my mind and has not left me since."

My heart rejoiced at seeing the Lord's faithfulness, but I thought it was better not to tell her about our circumstances, lest she would be influenced to give accordingly. If it was of the Lord, she would be moved to give. I turned the conversation to other subjects, but she gave me enough money to last all week. My wife and I were full of joy on account of the goodness of the Lord. He did not try our faith much at first, but allowed us to see His willingness to help us. Later, He tested our faith more fully.

The next Wednesday I went to Exmouth. Our money was again reduced to about nine shillings. I asked the Lord on Thursday to please give me some money. On Friday morning about eight o'clock, while in prayer, I was led to ask again for money. Before I rose from my knees, I felt fully assured that we would have the answer that same day. An hour later, I left the brother with whom I was staying, and he gave me some money. He said, "Take this for the expenses connected with your coming to us." I did not expect to have my expenses paid, but I saw the Lord's fatherly hand in this blessing.

When I came home about twelve o'clock, I asked my wife whether she had received any letters. She told me she had received one the day before from a brother who sent three sovereigns. Thus, even my prayer on the preceding day had been answered. The next day one of the brethren came and brought me four pounds which was due to me as a part of my former salary. I did not even know that this sum was due to me. Within thirty hours, in answer to prayer, I received seven pounds ten shillings.

Throughout 1830, the Lord richly supplied all my temporal needs, although I could not depend upon any human for a single shilling. Even regarding temporal things, I had lost nothing by acting according to the dictates of my conscience. In spiritual things, the Lord dealt bountifully with me and used me as an instrument in doing His work.

On the 6th, 7th, and 8th of January 1831, I repeatedly asked the Lord for money but received none. A few times I was tempted to distrust the Lord, although He had been so gracious to us. Up to this time, He had not only supplied all our needs but had given us many miraculous answers to prayer. I began to think it would be of no use to trust in the Lord this time. Perhaps I had gone too far in living by faith.

But praise the Lord! This trial lasted only a few minutes. He enabled me to trust in Him, and Satan was immediately defeated. When I returned to my room only ten minutes later, the Lord sent deliverance. A sister brought us two pounds four shillings. The Lord triumphed, and our faith was strengthened.

When we again had only a few shillings, we were given five pounds from the offering box. I had asked the brethren to please let me have the money in the box every week. But they either forgot to take it out weekly or were ashamed to bring such small sums. It was generally taken out every three to five weeks. I explained to them that I desired to look neither to man nor the box but to God. Therefore, I decided not to remind them of my request to have the money weekly, lest it hinder the testimony I wished to give of trusting in God alone.

On January 28, we had little money again although I had seen a brother open the box and take out the money four days earlier. But I would not ask him to let me have it. When the coals for our fire were almost gone, I asked the Lord to incline the brother's heart to bring the money to us. Shortly afterward, it was given to us, and our temporal needs were supplied.

The Lord has kept me from speaking, either directly or indirectly, about my needs. In a few instances I have spoken to very poor brethren to encourage them to trust in the Lord, telling them that I had to do the same.

On February 14 we again had very little money, and I asked the Lord to supply our needs. *The instant that I got up from my knees,* a brother gave me one pound which had been taken out of the box.

In March I was again tempted to doubt the faithfulness of the Lord. Although I was not worried about money, I was not fully resting upon Him so that I could triumph with joy. *One hour later* the Lord gave me another proof of His faithful love. A Christian lady brought five sovereigns for us, with these words written on paper: "I was hungry and ye gave me meat; I was thirsty, and ye gave me drink."

On the morning of April 16 our money was reduced to three shillings. I said to myself, "I must now go and ask the Lord earnestly for fresh supplies." But before I had prayed, two pounds were sent from Exeter as proof that the Lord hears before we call.

Some may say that such a way of life leads a Christian away from the Lord and from caring about spiritual things. They say it may cause the mind to be occupied with questions like: "What shall I eat, what shall I drink, and what shall I wear?" I have experienced both ways and know that my present manner of living by trusting God for temporal things is connected with less care. Trusting the Lord for the supply of my temporal needs keeps me from anxious thoughts like: "Will my salary last and will I have enough for the next month?" In this freedom I am able to say, "My Lord is not limited. He knows my present situation, and He can supply all I need." Rather than causing anxiety, living by faith in God alone keeps my heart in perfect peace.

This way of living has often revived the work of grace in my heart when I began to grow spiritually cold. It also has brought me back again to the Lord after I had been backsliding. It is not possible to live in sin, and at the same time, by communion with God, draw down from heaven everything one needs for this life. Frequently, a fresh answer to prayer quickens my soul and fills me with great joy.

In June brother Craik and I went to Torquay to preach. When I came home, my wife had about three shillings left. We waited upon the Lord, but no money came. The next morning, we were still waiting on the Lord and looking for deliverance. We had only a little butter left for breakfast, sufficient for a visiting brother and a relative. We did not mention our circumstances to them so that they would not be made uncomfortable.

After the morning prayer meeting, our brother unexpectedly opened the offering box and gave me the money. He told me that he and his wife could not sleep last night because they thought that we might need money. I had repeatedly asked the Lord for the money but received nothing. But when I prayed that the Lord would impress it on the brother that we needed money, he opened the box and gave it to me.

One morning in November I suggested we pray

about our temporal needs. Just as we were about to pray, a parcel came from Exmouth. We asked the Lord for meat for dinner since we had no money to buy any. After prayer, we opened the parcel and found a ham!

My wife and I never went into debt because we believed it to be unscriptural according to Romans 13:8, "Owe no man any thing, but to love one another." Therefore, we have no bills with our tailor, butcher, or baker, but we pay for everything in cash. We would rather suffer need than contract debts. Thus, we always know how much we have, and how much we can give away. Many trials come upon the children of God on account of not acting according to Romans 13:8.

November 27 was the Lord's day. Our money had been reduced to two pence. Our bread was hardly enough for the day. I brought our need before the Lord several times. When I gave thanks after lunch, I asked Him to give us our daily bread, meaning literally that He would send us bread for the evening. While I was praying, there was a knock at the door. A poor sister came in and brought us some of her dinner and five shillings. Later, she also brought us a large loaf of bread. Thus, the Lord not only gave us bread but also money.

At the end of the year, we looked back and realized that all our needs had been met more abundantly than if I had received a regular salary. We are never losers from doing the will of the Lord. I

43

have not served a hard Master, and that is what I delight to show.

God was also faithful to heal my physical infirmities. One Saturday afternoon, I broke a blood vessel in my stomach and lost a considerable quantity of blood. Immediately after I prayed, I began to feel better. Two brethren called on me to ask what arrangement should be made for a preacher at the Sunday services. I asked them to come again in about an hour when I would give them an answer.

After they were gone, the Lord gave me faith to get out of bed. I dressed and decided to go to the chapel. Walking the short distance to the chapel was an exertion to me in my weakened condition, but I preached that morning with a loud and strong voice for the usual length of time.

After the morning meeting, my doctor called on me and told me not to preach again in the afternoon because I could greatly injure myself. I told him that I would consider it great presumption if the Lord had not given me the faith to do it. That afternoon I preached again, and he called and said the same concerning the evening meeting. Nevertheless, having faith, I preached in the evening. After each meeting I became stronger, which was plain proof that the hand of God was in the matter.

The next day, the Lord enabled me to rise early in the morning and go to our usual prayer meeting where I read, spoke, and prayed. Later I wrote four letters, studied the Scriptures at home, and attended the meeting again in the evening. My health improved every day. I attended the two meetings as usual, preached in the evening, and did my other work besides. In less than a week, I was as well as I was before I broke the blood vessel.

Do not attempt to imitate me in this matter if you do not have the faith. But if you do, it will most assuredly be honored by God. I often prayed with sick believers until they were restored. When I ask the Lord for the blessing of bodily health, my request almost always is granted. In answer to my prayers, I was immediately restored from a bodily infirmity which had afflicted me for a long time, and it has never returned since.

Chapter 6

BEGINNING THE MINISTRY AT BRISTOL

For several months, I have been feeling that my work at Teignmouth would soon be completed. This feeling has continued to grow, and I am now convinced that Teignmouth is no longer my place of ministry. Perhaps my gift is going from place to place, seeking to bring believers back to the Scriptures, rather than staying in one place and laboring as a pastor. Wherever I go, I preach with much more enjoyment and power than at Teignmouth. Moreover, almost everywhere I have many more hearers than at Teignmouth and find the people hungering after spiritual food which is no longer the case at Teignmouth.

April 13. I received a letter from brother Craik from Bristol inviting me to come and help him. It appears to me that a place like Bristol would suit my gifts better. Lord, teach me! I feel more than ever that I will soon leave Teignmouth. But I fear that much connected with this decision is of the flesh. It seems to me that I will soon go to Bristol, if the Lord permits. I wrote a letter to brother Craik and promised to come, if I clearly see it is the Lord's will.

April 15. This evening I preached on the Lord's second coming. I told the brethren what effect this doctrine had upon me, and how it encouraged me to leave London and to preach throughout the land. The Lord had kept me at Teignmouth for these two years and three months, and it seemed that the time was near when I should leave. I reminded them of what I told them when they requested me to become their pastor—that I could stay only as long as I saw it was the Lord's will to do so. There was much weeping afterward, but I am now again in peace.

April 16. I am glad I have spoken to the brethren so that they may be prepared in case the Lord leads me to leave. I left today for Dartmouth and preached there in the evening. I had five answers to prayer today. 1. I awoke at five, a request I made of the Lord last evening. 2. The Lord removed an illness from my dear wife. It would have been difficult for me to leave her in that condition. 3. The Lord sent us money. 4. There was room for me on the Dartmouth coach. 5. This evening I was assisted in preaching, and my soul was refreshed.

I must offer a word of warning to believers. Often the work of the Lord itself may tempt us away from communion with Him. A full schedule of preaching, counseling, and travel can erode the strength of the mightiest servant of the Lord. Public prayer will never make up for closet communion.

After this evening's meeting, I should have withdrawn from the company of the brothers and sisters, explaining that I needed secret communion with the Lord. Instead, I spent the time until the coach came in conversation with them. Although I enjoyed their fellowship, my soul needed food. Without it, I was lean and felt the effects of it the whole day. I was even silent on the coach and did not speak a word for Christ or give away a single tract.

April 22. This morning I preached at Gideon Chapel in Bristol. In the afternoon I preached at the Pithay Chapel where a young man was converted. He was a notorious drunkard on his way to a tavern when an acquaintance met him and asked him to go to hear a foreigner preach. He did, and from that moment he was completely changed and never went to another tavern. His wife later told me that he was so happy in the Lord that he often neglected his supper to read the Scriptures instead.

Brother Craik's evening sermon spoke to my heart. I am now fully persuaded that Bristol is the place where the Lord will have me labor. But we are going home next week in order that in quietness, without being influenced by what we see here, we may seek the Lord's will concerning us.

April 29. As we sought the Lord, He helped us to see that He is sending us to Bristol!

April 30. Leaving the dear children of God in Teignmouth was difficult for me. Dozens begged us to return soon, many with tears in their eyes. The Lord has given a great blessing to our ministry. It was the Lord's will for us to come here for a time.

May 5. One other striking proof that leaving Teignmouth is of God is that some truly spiritual brothers, although they want me to stay, sincerely believe that I am called to go to Bristol.

May 15. While I was in prayer concerning Bristol, brother Craik sent for me. The congregation at Gideon Chapel have accepted our offer to come under the conditions we made. For the present, we wanted them to consider us only as ministering among them, but not in any fixed pastoral relationship. Thus we may preach the Word as the Spirit leads us. Regular salaries should be done away with, and we will go on trusting God to supply our needs. We intend, the Lord willing, to leave in about a week, although there is nothing settled about Bethesda Chapel.

May 21. Today I began to say goodbye to the brethren at Teignmouth, calling on each of them. It has been a trying day, filled with much weeping. If I was not fully persuaded that God wants us to go to Bristol, I would have hardly been able to bear it.

May 22. Some of the brethren at Teignmouth say that they expect us back again. As far as I understand the way God deals with His children, this seems unlikely. The Lord, after repeated prayer, gave me Colossians 1:21-23 as a text for my last word of exhortation to them. It seemed best to me to speak as little as possible about myself and as much as possible about Christ. I scarcely alluded to our separation and only commended myself and the brethren, in the concluding prayer, to the Lord. Parting scenes are very trying, but I am convinced that the separation is of the Lord.

May 23. My wife, my father-in-law, and I left this morning for Exeter. Dear brother Craik intends to follow us tomorrow. Just before we left Teignmouth, we unexpectedly received enough money to defray all the moving expenses. The Lord has confirmed His will concerning us going to Bristol many times.

May 27. We arrived at Bristol two days ago. This morning we received a sovereign from a sister in Teignmouth. The Lord will provide for us here also.

May 28. We spoke to the brethren who manage the finances at Gideon Chapel about receiving the free-will offerings through a box—a matter which was not quite settled with them. The Lord had graciously ordered this matter for us, and they did not object.

June 4. For several days we have been looking for lodging but found none plain and cheap enough. We began to make this a matter of earnest prayer. Immediately afterward, the Lord gave us a suitable place. It was particularly difficult to find an inexpensive, furnished place with five rooms which we need since brother Craik and we live together. How good the Lord is to have answered our prayer, and what an encouragement to commit everything to Him in prayer!

June 25. Today it was finally settled that we may take Bethesda Chapel for a year. A brother paid our rent with the understanding that, if the Lord blesses our labors in that place, the other believers will help him with the expenses. But if not, he will pay it all. This was the only way we could agree to take the chapel. If we would have had to go into debt, we could not think it was of God to minister in this place.

July 6. Today we began preaching at Bethesda Chapel. It was a good day.

July 16. This evening from six to nine o'clock, we made appointments to talk with individuals about salvation. These meetings are beneficial in many ways. Many people prefer coming at an appointed time to the church office to converse with us. Appointing a time for counseling with them in private concerning the things of eternity has brought some who never would have called upon us under other circumstances.

These appointments have also been a great encouragement to us in the work. Often when we thought that our teaching of the Word had done no good at all, we found the opposite was true as we counseled with people. We have been encouraged to go forward in the work of the Lord after seeing the many ways the Lord has used us as His instruments. Individuals have told us about the help they derived from our ministry even as long as four years ago.

Other servants of Christ, especially those who live in large towns, should consider setting apart time for seeing inquirers into the faith. These appointments, however, require much prayer for wisdom to speak with sensitivity to all those who come. We are not sufficient in our own ability for these things, but our sufficiency is from God. The appointments have been by far the most exhausting part of all our work, although at the same time the most rewarding.

July 18. I spent the whole morning in my office to have a quiet time with the Lord. This is the only way, on account of my numerous engagements, to make sure that I have time for prayer, reading the Word, and meditation.

September 17. This morning the Lord, in addition to all His other mercies, has given us our first child—a little girl. She and my wife are both doing well.

October 1. Many more people have been convicted of sin through brother Craik's preaching than my own. This is probably because brother Craik is more spiritually minded than I am, and he prays more earnestly for the conversion of sinners than I do. He addresses sinners in his public ministry frequently. This led me to more earnest prayer for the conversion of sinners. Since then, the Lord has used me as an instrument of conversion much more often.

May 28, 1833. Most of the Lord's people whom we know in Bristol are poor. This morning, while sitting in my room, the distress of several of the brethren was brought to my mind. I said to myself, "If only the Lord would give me the means to help them!" About an hour later, I received sixty pounds which I used to buy bread for the poor.

May 29. During the last twelve months of our labors in Bristol, one hundred and nine people have been added to our fellowship. Sixty-five have been converted, many backsliders have returned, and many of the children of God have been encouraged and strengthened in the way of truth.

June 12. This morning I felt that we should do something for the poor. We have given bread to them daily for some time now. I longed to establish a school for the boys and girls, read the Scriptures to them, and speak to them about the Lord. The chief obstacle was the pressure of work coming upon brother Craik and me at that time.

The number of the poor who came for bread had increased to between sixty and eighty a day. Our neighbors were annoyed because the beggars were loitering in the street. We had to tell them to no longer come for bread, but our desire to help these people has not diminished.

December 17. This evening brother Craik and I had tea with a family of five who had been brought to the Lord through our ministry. As an encouragement to anyone who may desire to preach the gospel in a foreign language, I must mention that the first member of this family who was converted came merely out of curiosity to hear my foreign accent.

December 31. At least 260 people have met with us about the concerns of their souls. Out of these, 153 have been added to us in fellowship these last eighteen months, sixty of whom have been brought to the knowledge of the Lord through our preaching and prayers.

Four years have passed since I began to trust in the Lord alone for the supply of my temporal needs. All I had then at most was worth one hundred pounds a year. I gave it up for the Lord and had nothing left but about five pounds. The Lord greatly honored this little sacrifice and gave me considerably more in return.

During the last three years and three months, I never have asked anyone for anything. The Lord has graciously supplied all my needs as I bring them to Him. At the close of each of these four years, although my income has been comparatively great, I have had only a few shillings left. My needs are met each day by the help of God.

Chapter 7

THE SCRIPTURAL KNOWLEDGE INSTITUTION

January 9, 1834. During these past eighteen months, brother Craik and I have preached once a month at Brislington, a village near Bristol. We had not seen any fruit from our labors there. This led me to pray earnestly to the Lord for the conversion of sinners in that place. I asked the Lord to convert at least one soul this evening so that we might have a little encouragement. Tonight a young man was brought to the knowledge of the truth.

February 21. I began to form a plan to establish an institution for the spread of the gospel at home and abroad. I trust this matter is of God.

February 25. I was led again today to pray about forming a new missionary institution and felt more certain that we should do so. Some people may ask why we formed a new institution for the spread of the gospel and why we did not unite with some of the religious societies already in existence. I give, therefore, our reasons in order to show that nothing but the desire to maintain a good conscience led us to act as we have.

The Word of God is the only rule of action for the disciples of the Lord Jesus. In comparing the existing religious societies with the Word of God, we found that they departed so far from it that we could not be united with them and maintain a good conscience.

The goal which these religious societies are working toward is that the whole world will eventually be converted. They refer to the passage in Habakkuk 2:14, "For the earth shall be filled with the knowledge of the glory of the Lord, as the waters cover the sea;" or the one in Isaiah 11:9, "For the earth shall be full of the knowledge of the Lord, as the waters cover the sea."

These passages have no reference to the present dispensation but to the one which will begin when the Lord returns. In the present time, things will not become spiritually better, but worse. Only people gathered out from among the Gentiles for the Lord will be converted. This is clear from many passages in God's Word. (See Matthew 13:24-30, 36-43; 2 Timothy 3:1-13; Acts 15:14.) A hearty desire and earnest prayer for the conversion of sinners is quite scriptural. But it is unscriptural to expect the conversion of the whole world. We could not set such a goal for ourselves in the service of the Lord.

But even worse is the connection of those religious societies with the world. In temporal things, the children of God must make use of the world but the work to be done requires that those who attend to it should have spiritual life (of which unbelievers are utterly destitute). The children of God are bound by their loyalty to their Lord to refrain from any association with the unregenerate.

The connection with the world is obvious in these religious societies, for everyone who donates a certain amount is considered to be a member. Although such an individual may live in sin; although he may manifest to everyone that he does not know the Lord Jesus; if only the money is paid, he is a member and has a right to vote. Moreover, whoever pays a larger sum can be a member for life, however openly sinful his life is. Surely such things ought not to be.

The methods used in these religious societies to obtain money for the work of the Lord are also unscriptural. It is common to ask the unconverted for money, which even Abraham would not have done. (See Genesis 14:21-24.) How much less should we do it! We are forbidden to have fellowship with unbelievers in all such matters because we are in fellowship with the Father and the Son. We can, therefore, obtain everything from the Lord we can possibly need in His service without being obliged to go to the unconverted world. The first disciple did this in 3 John 7—"Because that for his name's sake they went forth, taking nothing of the Gentiles."

The individuals who manage the affairs of the societies may be unconverted persons or even open enemies to the truth. This is permitted because they are rich or influential. I have never known a case of a poor, but wise and experienced, servant of Christ being invited to lead such public meetings. Surely the Galilean fishermen or even our Lord Himself would not have been called to this office according to these principles. The disciples of the Lord Jesus should not judge a person's fitness for service in the Church by the position he fills in the world or by the wealth he possesses.

Almost all these societies contract debts so that it is rare to read a report of any of them without finding that they have expended more than they have received. This is contrary both to the spirit and to the letter of the New Testament. "Owe no man any thing, but to love one another" (Romans 13:8).

Brother Craik and I heartily agree that many true children of God are connected with these religious societies. The Lord has blessed their efforts in many ways, despite the existence of practices we judge to be unscriptural. Yet it appeared to us to be His will that we should be separate from these societies.

By the blessing of God, we may help the children of God in those societies to realize their unscriptural practices. We remained united in brotherly love with the individual believers belonging to them. We would by no means judge them if they do not see that their practices are contrary to Scripture. But since we see them to be so ourselves, we could not with a clear conscience remain.

We thought that it would be harmful to the brethren among whom we labored if we did nothing to support missionary work. Therefore, we wanted to do something to spread the gospel at home and abroad, however small the beginning might be.

March 5. This evening at a public meeting, brother Craik and I stated the principles on which we intend to establish our institution for the spread of the gospel at home and abroad. There was nothing outwardly impressive either in the number of people present or in our speeches. May the Lord graciously grant His blessing upon the institution which will be called The Scriptural Knowledge Institution for Home and Abroad.

The Principles Of The Institution

1. We consider every believer to be called to help the cause of Christ, and we have scriptural reasons to expect the Lord's blessing on our work of faith and labor of love. The world will not be converted before the coming of our Lord Jesus, but while He tarries, all scriptural means should be employed for the ingathering of the elect of God.

2. With the Lord's help, we will not seek the

patronage of the world. We never intend to ask unconverted people of rank or wealth to support this institution because we believe this would be dishonorable to the Lord. "In the name of our God we will set up our banners" (Psalm 20:5). He alone will be our patron. If He helps us we will prosper; and if He is not on our side, we will not succeed.

3. We will not ask unbelievers for money although we will accept their contributions if they offer them of their own accord. (See Acts 28:2-10.)

4. We reject the help of unbelievers in managing or carrying on the affairs of the institution. (See 2 Corinthians 6:14-18.)

5. We intend never to enlarge the field of labor by contracting debts and then appealing to the Church for help. This is contrary both to the letter and the spirit of the New Testament. In secret prayer, God helping us, we will carry the needs of the institution to the Lord and act according to the direction that God gives.

6. We will not measure the success of the institution by the amount of money given or the number of Bibles distributed, but by the Lord's blessing on the work. "Not by might, nor by power, but my spirit, saith the Lord of hosts" (Zechariah 4:6). We expect His blessing in proportion to our waiting upon Him in prayer.

7. While we avoid needless separation, we desire to go on simply according to Scripture,

without compromising the truth. We will thankfully receive any scriptural instruction which experienced believers, after prayer, may have to give us concerning the institution.

The Goals Of The Institution

1. We will assist day schools, Sunday schools, and adult schools which give instruction on scriptural principles. As the Lord supplies the finances and suitable teachers and makes our path clear, we will establish schools of this kind. We also intend to place poor children into such day schools.

a. Our day school teachers must be godly people, the way of salvation must be scripturally pointed out, and no instruction may oppose the principles of the gospel.

b. Our Sunday school teachers must be believers and the Holy Scriptures alone will be the foundation of instruction. We consider it unscriptural that any people who do not know the Lord themselves should be allowed to give religious instruction.

c. The institution will not provide any adult school with the supply of Bibles, Testaments, or spelling books unless the teachers are believers.

2. We will distribute the Holy Scriptures.

3. We will assist missionaries whose ministry appears to be carried out according to the Scriptures.

March 7. Today we have only one shilling left. This evening when we came home from our work, we found our tailor waiting for us. He brought a new suit of clothes for brother Craik and me, which another brother had ordered for us.

April 23. Yesterday and today I asked the Lord to send us twenty pounds, that we might be able to purchase a larger stock of Bibles and Testaments than our small fund would allow. This evening a sister, unasked, promised to give us that sum. She added that she felt a particular joy in circulating the Holy Scriptures because reading the Word had brought her to the knowledge of the Lord.

June 8. I obtained no text for my sermon this morning despite repeated prayer and reading of the Word. When I awoke, these words were on my mind: "My grace is sufficient for thee." As soon as I dressed, I turned to 2 Corinthians 12 to consider this passage. But after prayer, I decided that I had not been directed to this portion for the sake of speaking on it, as I at first thought.

Therefore, I followed my usual practice in such cases—I continued reading the Scriptures where I left off last evening. When I came to Hebrews 11:13-16, I felt that this was the text. Having prayed, I was confirmed in it, and the Lord opened this passage to me. I preached on it with great enjoyment. God greatly blessed what I said, and at least one soul was brought to the Lord.

June 25. These last three days I have had very

little real communion with God, and have therefore been irritable and weak spiritually.

June 26. I rose early this morning and spent nearly two hours in prayer before breakfast. I now feel more comfortable.

July 11. I have prayed much about a director for the boys' school which will be established in connection with our little institution. Eight have applied for the position, but none seemed to be suitable. Now, at last, the Lord has given us a brother who will begin the work.

October 9. Our institution, established in dependence upon the Lord, has now been in operation for seven months. Many have been benefited with instruction. In the Sunday school we have about 120 children; in the adult school, about 40 adults; in the day schools, 209 children. We have circulated 482 Bibles and 520 New Testaments. Lastly, a sizable amount has been spent to aid missionary work.

October 28. We heard a moving account of a poor little orphan boy who for some time attended one of our schools. He was recently taken to the poorhouse some miles outside of Bristol. He expressed great sorrow that he could no longer attend our school and ministry. May this lead me to do something to supply the temporal needs of poor children, the pressure of which has caused this poor boy to be taken away from our school!

November 4. I spent most of the morning reading the Word and in prayer. I also asked for our daily bread, for we have scarcely any money left.

November 5. I spent almost the whole day in prayer and reading the Word. I prayed again for the supply of our temporal needs, but the Lord has not yet answered.

November 8. The Lord has graciously again supplied our temporal needs during this week, although at the beginning of it we had little left. I have prayed much this week for money, more than any other week since we have been in Bristol. The Lord has provided through people paying what they owed us. We also sold some of the things that we did not need.

December 31. Since brother Craik and I have been laboring in Bristol, 227 brothers and sisters have been added to us in fellowship. Out of these, 103 have been converted, and many have been brought into the liberty of the gospel or reclaimed from backsliding. Forty-seven young converts are at Gideon and fifty-six at Bethesda.

January 1, 1835. Last evening we had a special prayer meeting to praise the Lord for His many mercies which we have received during the past year. We asked Him to continue to show us His favor.

January 13. I visited from house to house the people living on Orange Street, to find out whether any individuals wanted Bibles, whether they could read, and whether they wanted their children placed in our day schools or Sunday school. This gave me many opportunities to converse with them about their souls.

January 15. This morning I went again from house to house on Orange Street. I greatly delight in such work, for it is very important; but my hands are so full with other work that I can do little of it.

January 21. I received, in answer to prayer, five pounds for the Scriptural Knowledge Institution. The Lord pours in, while we continue to pour out. During the past week, fifty-eight copies of the Scriptures were sold at reduced prices. We want to continue this important work, but we will require much financial help.

January 28. For these past few days, I have prayed much about whether the Lord will have me to go as a missionary to the East Indies. I am willing to go if He wants to use me in this way.

January 29. I have been greatly stirred to pray about going to Calcutta as a missionary. May the Lord guide me in this matter!

February 25. In the name of the Lord and in dependence on Him alone for support, we have established a fifth day school for poor children, which opened today. We now have two boys' schools and three girls' schools.

June 3. Today we held a public meeting on account of the Scriptural Knowledge Institution for Home and Abroad. For the past fifteen months we have been able to provide poor children with schooling, circulate the Holy Scriptures, and aid missionary labors.

During this time, although the field of labor has been continually enlarging and although we have at times been brought low in funds, the Lord has never allowed us to stop the work. We have established three day schools and two other charity day schools, which otherwise would have been closed for lack of funds.

The number of children that have been provided with schooling in the day schools amounts to 439. The number of copies of the Holy Scriptures which have been circulated is 795 Bibles and 753 New Testaments. We have also sent aid to missionary labors in Canada, the East Indies, and on the continent of Europe.

June 25. Our little boy is so ill that I have no hope of his recovery.

June 26. My prayer last evening was that God would support my dear wife under the trial. Two hours later, the little one went home to be with the Lord. I fully realize that the dear infant is much better off with the Lord Jesus than with us, and when I weep, I weep for joy.

July 18. I have felt weak in my chest for several days. Today I felt it more than ever, and think it would be wise to refrain next week from all public speaking. May the Lord grant that I may be brought nearer to Him through this.

July 31. Today a former minister came to us and began to go from house to house to spread the truth as a city missionary. This was a divine appointment. Brother Craik had for some months been unable, on account of illness, to labor in the work of the schools and the circulation of the Scriptures. My own weakness increased so that I was obliged to give up the work entirely. How gracious, therefore, of the Lord to send our brother that the work might go on!

August 24. I feel very weak and suffer more than ever from the disease. Should I leave Bristol for a while? I have no money to go away to recover. A sister in the country invited me to visit for a week, and I may accept the invitation and go tomorrow.

August 26. Today I had five pounds given to me for the purpose of going away to recover.

August 29. Today I received another five pounds for the same purpose.

August 30. Today, for the first Sunday since our arrival in Bristol, I have been kept from preaching because of illness. How mercifully the Lord has dealt in giving me so much strength for these years! Another five pounds were sent to me today. How kind the Lord is to provide me with the money to leave Bristol!

September 19. I received a kind letter from a brother and two sisters in the Lord who live on the Isle of Wight. They invited me to come and stay with them for some time. In addition to this, they wrote that they had repeatedly prayed about the matter and were persuaded that I ought to come.

The Lord graciously provided the money so that my family and I could travel there for the rest that we needed.

September 29. Last evening when I said good-night to the family, I wanted to go to sleep at once. The weakness in my body and the coldness of the night tempted me to pray no longer. However, the Lord helped me to kneel before Him. No sooner had I begun to pray than His Spirit shone into my soul and gave me such a spirit of prayer as I had not enjoyed for many weeks. He graciously revived His work in my heart. I enjoyed that nearness to God and fervency in prayer for more than an hour. My soul had been panting for many weeks for this sweet experience.

For the first time during this illness, I asked the Lord earnestly to restore me to health. I now long to go back to the work in Bristol, yet I am not impatient. The Lord will strengthen me to return to it. I went to bed especially happy and awoke this morning in great peace. For more than an hour, I had real communion with the Lord before breakfast. May He in mercy continue this state of heart to His most unworthy child!

November 15. We arrived safely in Bristol. Last week we prayed repeatedly concerning the work of the Scriptural Knowledge Institution and especially that the Lord would give us the means to continue and even enlarge the work. In addition to this, I have asked for my own needs to be met and

He has kindly granted both these requests. May I have grace to trust Him more and more!

Chapter 8

PROVING GOD'S FAITHFULNESS

November 21. Today it has been impressed on my heart no longer merely to think about establishing an orphan house but actually to begin making plans. I spent much time in prayer to find the Lord's will in this situation.

November 23. The Lord, in answer to prayer, has given me about fifty pounds. I had asked only for forty pounds. This has been a great encouragement to me and has stirred me to think and pray even more about establishing an orphan house.

November 25. I again spent much time in prayer yesterday and today about the orphan house. I am convinced that it is of God. May He in mercy guide me!

There are several reasons why I desire to establish an orphan house. One of the things the children of God need most is to have their faith strengthened. I visited a brother who worked fourteen to sixteen hours a day at his trade. His body ached, his soul was lean, and he had no joy in God.

I pointed out to him that he should work less in order that his health might not suffer. He could gather strength for his inner man by reading the Word of God, by meditation on it, and by prayer.

He replied, "But if I work less, I do not earn enough for the support of my family. Even now, while I work so much, I have scarcely enough."

He had no trust in God and no real belief in the truth of that word, "Seek ye first the kingdom of God, and his righteousness; and all these things shall be added unto you" (Matthew 6:33).

I explained to him, "My dear brother, it is not your work which supports your family, but the Lord. He has fed you and your family when you could not work at all because of illness. He would surely provide for you and yours, if, for the sake of obtaining food for your inner man, you worked fewer hours a day to give you proper time for rest. You begin to work after only a few hurried moments for prayer. You leave your work in the evening and intend to read a little of the Word of God, but by then you are too worn out in body and mind to enjoy it. You often fall asleep while reading the Scriptures or while on your knees in prayer."

The brother admitted this was true. He agreed that my advice was good, but I read in his countenance, even if he did not actually say so, "How could I make ends meet if I were to carry out your advice?" I longed to have something to give the brother as a visible proof that our God and Father is the same faithful God that He ever was. He is willing as ever to prove Himself the living God to all who put their trust in Him.

Sometimes children of God are fearful of growing old and being unable to work any longer. If I point out to them how their heavenly Father has always helped those who put their trust in Him, they might not *say* that times have changed. But it is evident that they do not see God as the *living* God. I longed to set something before the children of God that they might see that He does not forsake, even in hard times, those who rely on Him.

Christian businessmen suffer in their spiritual lives and bring guilt on their consciences by carrying on their business in the same way that unconverted people do. The competition in trade, bad times, and overpopulation are given as reasons why a business carried on according to the Word of God could not be expected to prosper. Few people have the holy determination to trust in the living God and depend on Him in order that a good conscience might be maintained. I want to show these people that God is faithful and can be trusted without reservation.

Some individuals are in professions which they cannot continue with a good conscience. But they fear leaving their profession lest they become unemployed. I long to strengthen their faith by proving that the promises from the Word of God of His willingness and ability to help all those who rely on Him are true.

I know that the Word of God ought to be enough. But by giving my brothers visible proof of the unchangeable faithfulness of the Lord, I might strengthen their faith. I want to be the servant of the Church in the particular point on which I had obtained mercy—in being able to take God at His Word and to rely on it.

This seems to me best done by establishing an orphan house—something which could be seen by the natural eye. If I, a poor man, simply by prayer and faith obtained, without asking any individual, the finances for establishing and carrying on an orphan house, this might strengthen the faith of the children of God. It would also be a testimony to the unconverted of the reality of the things of God.

This is the primary reason for establishing the orphan house. I certainly desire to be used by God to help the poor children and train them in the ways of God. But the primary object of the work is that God would be magnified because the orphans under my care will be provided with all they need through prayer and faith. Everyone will see that God is faithful and hears prayer.

November 28. I have been praying every day this week concerning the orphan house, entreating the Lord to take away every thought of it if the matter is not of Him. After repeatedly examining the motives of my heart, I am convinced that it is of God.

December 2. Brother Craik and I have talked

about the orphan house. I wanted him to show me any hidden corruption of my heart or any other scriptural reason against engaging in it. The only reason I could doubt that it is of God for me to begin this work is the numerous responsibilities which I have already. But if the matter is of God, He will, in due time, send suitable individuals so that comparatively little of my time will be taken up in this service.

Brother Craik greatly encouraged me in the work. Today I took the first step in the matter and announced a public meeting on December 9. The brethren want to hear my thoughts concerning the orphan house, and I want to know the Lord's will more clearly.

December 5. This Scripture came alive to me today: "Open thy mouth wide, and I will fill it" (Psalm 81:10). I was led to apply it to the orphan house and asked the Lord for a building, one thousand pounds, and suitable individuals to take care of the children.

December 7. Today I received the first shilling for the orphan house.

December 9. This afternoon the first piece of furniture was given—a large wardrobe. I felt low in spirit about the orphan house, but as soon as I began to speak at the evening meeting, I received assistance from God. After the meeting, ten shillings were given to me. There was no collection taken, nor did anyone speak besides myself. The meeting was not in the least intended to work upon people's emotions to gain support. After the meeting, a sister offered herself for the work. I went home happy in the Lord and full of confidence that the matter will come to pass, although only ten shillings have been given.

December 10. I received a letter from a brother and sister who wrote, "We offer ourselves for the service of the intended orphan house, if you think we are qualified for it. Also we will give up all the furniture and household items which the Lord has given us, for its use. We do this without expecting any salary, believing that if it is the will of the Lord to employ us, He will supply all our need."

During the next several weeks, God answered our prayers concerning the orphan house. We were given furniture, fabric, kitchen utensils, blankets, plates, and cups, in addition to financial support. Some days very little came in, and I would begin to feel discouraged. But the Lord strengthened me during those times and touched the hearts of others to abundantly supply our needs. Several other people offered their services to work among the orphans, completely trusting God for their support.

One sister in particular was a great source of blessing to me as she gave generously although she had little. She earned only a few shillings a week as a seamstress. When her father died, he left her four hundred pounds. She paid off the substantial debts he had contracted, gave one hundred pounds to her mother, and brought another hundred pounds to me for the work of the orphan house.

Before accepting the money, I had a long conversation with her. I needed to know her motives, and whether she might have given this money emotionally, without having counted the cost. But I had not conversed long with this beloved sister before I found that she was a quiet, calm, considerate follower of the Lord Jesus. She desired, in spite of what human reasoning might say, to act according to the words of our Lord, "Lay not up for yourselves treasures upon earth" (Matthew 6:19). "Sell that ye have, and give alms" (Luke 12:33).

When I continued questioning her in order that I might see whether she had counted the cost, she said to me, "The Lord Jesus gave His last drop of blood for me. Should I not give Him the hundred pounds?"

Four things must be noticed about this beloved sister. 1. She did all these things in secret and thus proved that she did not desire the praise of man. 2. She remained, as before, of an humble and lowly mind. She gave her money for the Lord and not to impress man. 3. During all the time that she had this comparative abundance, she did not change her lodging, dress, or manner of life. She remained in every way the poor handmaiden of the Lord to all outward appearance. 4. She continued to work at her sewing all this time, earning three shillings or a little more a week while she gave away the money in five-pound notes.

At last all her money was gone several years before her death. She found herself completely dependent upon the Lord, who never forsook her, up to the last moments of her earthly life. Her body grew weaker, and she was able to work very little. But the Lord supplied her with all she needed, although she never asked for anything. For instance, a sister in our fellowship sent her all the bread she needed. She was full of thanksgiving, always praising the Lord.

April 2, 1836. This day was set apart for prayer and thanksgiving for the opening of the Orphan House. In the morning, several brethren prayed, and brother Craik spoke on the last verses of Psalm 20. I addressed our day and Sunday school children and the orphans; and in the evening, we had another prayer meeting. Seventeen children are living in the Orphan House.

May 16 For several weeks our income has been low. Although I prayed many times that the Lord would enable us to pay our taxes, the prayer remained unanswered. The Lord will send help by the time it is needed.

One thing particularly has been a trial to us lately, far more than our temporal circumstances. We have scarcely been able to relieve the poverty among the poor saints. Seven pounds twelve shillings were given to me as my part of the freewill offerings through the boxes, and two five-pound notes were put in yesterday—one for brother Craik and one for me. Thus the Lord has again delivered us and answered our prayers, *not one single hour too late*. The taxes are not yet due. May He fill my heart with gratitude for this fresh deliverance. May He enable me to trust more in Him and to wait patiently for His help!

Chapter 9

THE MINISTRY EXPANDS

May 18, 1836. The Lord has crowned the prayers of His servant concerning the establishment of an Orphan House with great success. My prayer was that He would graciously provide a house, either as a loan or as a gift, or that someone might be led to pay the rent for one. Furthermore, I asked that He would give me one thousand pounds for the work and suitable individuals to take care of the children. A day or two later, I asked that He would put it into the hearts of His people to send me articles of furniture and some clothes for the children.

In answer to these petitions, many articles of furniture, clothing, and food were sent. A conditional offer of a house, as a gift, was made, and several individuals offered to take care of the children. Various sums of money were also given, varying from one hundred pounds to a halfpenny. The above results have come in answer to prayer, without me asking anyone for one single thing. I did not keep silent about our needs on account of lack of confidence in the brethren or because I doubted their love for the Lord, but I wanted to see the hand of God much more clearly.

I brought even the most minute circumstances concerning the Orphan House before the Lord, being conscious of my own weakness and ignorance. One point I had never prayed about, however, was for the Lord to send more children. I took it for granted that there would be plenty of applications.

The appointed time came, and no applications were being made. This circumstance led me to bow low before my God in prayer and to examine the motives of my heart once more. I could still say that His glory was my chief aim—that others might see it is not a vain thing to trust in the living God.

Continuing in prayer, I was at last able to say from my heart that I would rejoice in God being glorified in this matter, even if it meant bringing the whole plan to nothing. But it still seemed more glorifying to God to establish and prosper the Orphan House. I then asked Him heartily to send applications.

I now enjoyed a peaceful state of heart concerning the subject and was also more assured than ever that God would establish the work. The very next day the first application was made, and within a short time forty-three more were received. I rented a house, which because of its cheapness and size, was very suitable.

We intended to take in children from seven to twelve years of age. But after six applications had been made for children between four and six years, it became a subject of solemn and prayerful consideration whether to accept these children as long as there were vacancies. I came at last to the conclusion to take in the little girls under seven years of age.

An Orphan House was needed for male children under seven years old also. Clothing was even sent for little boys. Since the Lord has done far above what I could have expected, I decided to establish an Infant Orphan House.

June 3. From May 16 up to this day, I have been confined to the house and a part of the time to my bed because of sickness. Almost every day during this time, I have been able to write a narrative of the Lord's dealings with me. My greatest objection against writing it for publication was a lack of time. Now, this affliction leaves my mind free and gives me time because I am confined to the house. I have written over one hundred pages.

June 14. This morning we prayed about the schools and the circulation of the Scriptures. Besides asking for blessings upon the work, we have also asked the Lord for the finances we need. The rent for the classrooms will be due on July 1, and we need at least forty pounds more to continue the circulation of the Scriptures, to pay the salaries of the teachers, and other expenses. We have only about seven pounds for all these needs. I also pray for the remainder of the thousand pounds for the Orphan House.

June 21. The Lord has sent us, through the offerings last week, the amount due for the rent of two classrooms. We even have five pounds more than is needed. Once more the Lord has answered our prayers.

July 28. We would not have been able to pay the weekly salary of the teachers had not the Lord helped us again today. This evening a brother gave eight pounds from a number of his workmen who paid weekly one penny each of their own accord toward our funds. The money had been collecting for many months, and, in this our time of need, it had been put into the heart of this brother to bring it.

October 1. In dependence upon the Lord alone for support, we hired a brother as a headmaster for a sixth day school. On account of the many deliverances which we have had lately, we have not hesitated to enlarge the work and another boys' school was greatly needed.

October 5. Twenty-five pounds was given to me for the Scriptural Knowledge Institution. The Lord has already given the means of defraying the expenses of the new boys' school for some months to come.

October 19. I have at last employed a sister as matron for the Infant Orphan House. Up to this day, I had never met an individual who seemed suitable, although money has been available for some time to begin this work. Applications have been made for several infant orphans.

October 25. By the kind hand of God, we have obtained suitable premises for the Infant Orphan House.

November 5. A brother gave one hundred pounds to pay our rent. In December of last year, I had repeatedly asked the Lord to incline the heart of this brother to give one hundred pounds. I made note of this prayer in my journal on December 12, 1835. On January 25, 1836, fifty pounds were promised by him, and on November 5, fifty pounds more were given. When I remembered that this prayer had been noted in my journal, I showed it to the donor. We rejoiced together—he to have been the instrument in giving, and I to have had the request granted.

November 30. On account of many pressing engagements, I have not prayed about the funds for some time. But being in great need, I was led to earnestly seek the Lord. In answer to this petition, a brother gave me ten pounds. He had it in his heart for several months to give this sum, but had been kept from it, not having the means. Now, in our time of great need, the Lord furnished him with the means, he used it to help us. In addition to this ten pounds, I received a letter with five pounds from a sister whom I never saw. She wrote, "It has been on my mind lately to send you some money, and I feel as if there must be some need. I, therefore, send you five pounds, all I have in the house at this moment.''

December 15. This day was set apart for prayer and thanksgiving regarding the Infant Orphan House, which was opened on November 28. In the morning we had a prayer meeting. In the afternoon, besides prayer and thanksgiving, I addressed the 350 children of our day schools and the orphans. Donations of money, food, clothes, books, and coal were received during the year. Also, we received offers of free medical care and supplies.

December 31. We had a prayer meeting to praise the Lord for His goodness during the past year and to ask Him to continue His favor toward us.

May 18, 1837. Sixty-four children now live in the two Orphan Houses. Two more are expected, and this will fill the two houses.

May 28. The narrative of some of the Lord's dealings with me is now ready to be published. I have asked the Lord to give me what is lacking of the one thousand pounds. In my own mind, the thing is as good as done, and I have repeatedly thanked God that He will surely give me every shilling of that sum. I earnestly desired that the book not leave the press until every shilling of that sum had been given in answer to prayer. Thus I might have the sweet privilege of bearing my testimony for God in this book.

June 15. I again prayed earnestly for the remainder of the thousand pounds. This evening, five pounds were given so that now the whole sum has been received. For the last eighteen months and ten days, I have brought this petition before God almost daily. From the moment I asked until the Lord granted it fully, I never doubted that He would give every shilling of that sum. Often I praised Him in the assurance that He would grant my request. When we pray, we must believe that we receive according to Mark 11:24, "What things soever ye desire, when ye pray, believe that ye receive them, and ye shall have them."

The Lord has listened to my prayers, and I believe He has given me a special gift of faith in His promises. An Orphan House for boys over seven years of age seems greatly needed in this city. Without it, we would not know how to provide for the little boys in the Infant Orphan House when they are older than seven years. Therefore, I plan to establish an Orphan House for about forty boys above seven years of age.

July 12. It is now three years and four months since Brother Craik and I began to spread the gospel through schools, circulate the Holy Scriptures, and aid missionaries. Since then we have distributed 4,030 copies of the Scriptures; four day schools for poor children have been established by us; 1,119 children have been instructed in the six day schools, and 353 children are now in those six day schools. Besides this, a Sunday school and an adult school have been supplied with all they needed. Missionary work in the East Indies, northern Canada, and Europe has been aided. In addition to this, the Word of God has been preached from house to house among the poor though the Scriptural Knowledge Institution.

August 15. The first edition of my book was published.

August 17. Two more children were received into the Infant Orphan House. Sixty-six children live in the Girl's and Infant's Orphan Houses.

September 2. I have been looking for a house for the orphan boys these last three days. Everything else has been provided. In His own time, the Lord will give us a house also.

September 19. It was particularly impressed on my heart that I need more rest although the ministry may suffer. Arrangements should be made so that I may be able to visit the brethren more because an unvisited church will sooner or later become an unhealthy church. Pastors and fellow-laborers are greatly needed among us.

September 28. I have for a long time been too busy. Yesterday morning I spent about three hours in the vestry of Gideon chapel to rest and pray. I meant to do the same in the afternoon, but before I could leave the house, someone came to talk to me. One person after the other came until I had to leave. It has been the same again today.

October 16. For a long time Brother Craik and I have realized the importance of more pastoral visiting. One of our greatest trials is that we have been unable to give more time to it. This evening we had a meeting of the two churches. Brother Craik and I and another brother from Devonshire spoke on the importance of pastoral visiting, the obstacles which hindered us, and whether there was any way of removing some of the obstacles.

Pastoral visiting is important for many reasons. Watching over the saints can help prevent backsliding as we counsel them in family, business, and spiritual matters. We want to keep up a loving and familiar communion with the people.

The particular obstacles in our case are:

1. The large number of people who are in communion with us. One hundred would be the most we would have strength to visit regularly. But there are nearly four hundred in fellowship with us.

2. The distance of the houses of the saints from our own homes. Many live more than two miles away.

3. The Lord's blessing on our labors. Not one year has passed since we have been in Bristol, without more than fifty being added to our number. Each of these people needed to be conversed with several times before being admitted into fellowship.

4. Brother Craik and I have the responsibility of two churches. At first glance, it appears as if the work is divided, but actually the double number of meetings means nearly double the work.

5. The care of a large body of believers takes much more time and requires much more strength than taking care of a small body of believers.

6. The position which we have in the church at large brings many brethren to us who travel through Bristol. They call on us or lodge with us, and we have to give them some of our time.

7. Extensive correspondence must be answered every day.

8. The physical weakness of both brother Craik and me is another hindrance. When the preaching is done; when strangers who lodge with us are gone; when the calls at our house are over; when the necessary letters, however briefly, are written; and when the church business is settled, our minds are often exhausted.

9. Even if we had strength remaining after we had taken care of all our other duties, our frame of mind is not always inclined toward visiting. After a trying day, one may be fit for the prayer closet, but not for visiting the saints.

10. Much of my time is taken up by the Orphan Houses, schools, circulation of the Scriptures, aiding missionary efforts, and other work connected with the Scriptural Knowledge Institution.

What is to be done under these circumstances? The Lord has not laid on us a burden which is too heavy, for He is not a hard Master. Perhaps He does not want us to attempt to visit all the saints as much as we believe is necessary.

We need other pastors; not nominal pastors, but

those whom the Lord has called, and to whom He has given a pastor's heart and pastoral gifts. These men may be raised up by the Lord from our own number, or the Lord may send them from elsewhere.

In order that time may be saved, it appears wise that the two churches, Bethesda and Gideon, should be united into one and that the number of weekly meetings should be reduced.

October 21. Today the Lord has given me a house for the Orphan Boys on the same street as the other two Orphan Houses.

December 31. In review of the year 1837, eighty-one children live in the three Orphan Houses, and nine workers care for them. Ninety people daily sit down to the table. Lord, look on the needs of Your servant!

The schools require even more help than before, particularly the Sunday school in which there are about 320 children. Lord, Your servant is a poor man, but I have trusted in You and made my boast in You before the sons of men. Do not let me fail in this work! Let it not be said all this was mere emotion and enthusiasm and will eventually come to nothing!

Chapter 10

PERSEVERING UNDER TRIAL

January 7, 1838. My general health seems to have improved, but this is the ninth's Lord's day that I have been unable to minister in the Word. My affliction causes me to be very irritable.

January 15. My headache has become less severe since yesterday afternoon. But I am still far from being well. God is purifying me for His blessed service, and I will soon be restored to the work. Also, He has restored a fervency of spirit which I have now enjoyed for the past three days. He has drawn my soul into real communion with Himself and into a holy desire to be more conformed to His dear Son.

When God gives a spirit of prayer, it is easy to pray! I spent about three hours in prayer over Psalms 64 and 65. In reference to that precious word, "O thou that hearest prayer" (Psalm 65:2), I asked the Lord the following petitions and entreated Him to record them in heaven and to answer them:

1. That He would give me grace to glorify Him by a submissive and patient spirit under my affliction.

2. That the work of conversion through Brother Craik and myself might not cease but go on as much now as when we first came to Bristol, and even more abundantly than then.

3. That He would give more spiritual prosperity to the church under our care than we have as yet enjoyed.

4. That His rich blessing would rest on this little work so that many may be converted through it and many benefited by it.

5. That He would bring salvation to all the children under our care.

6. That He would supply the means to carry on these institutions and to enlarge them.

I believe God has heard my prayers. He will make it manifest in His own good time that He has heard me. I have recorded my petitions that when God has answered them, His name will be glorified.

January 16. How very good is the Lord! Fervency of spirit, through His grace, is continued to me, although this morning, if not for the help of God, I would have lost it again. The weather has been very cold for several days, but today I felt it more, due to the weakness of my body.

I arose from my knees and stirred the fire, but I still felt very cold. I moved to another part of the room but felt even colder. At last, having prayed for some time, I decided to walk to help my circulation.

I entreated the Lord that this circumstance might not rob me of the precious communion I have had with Him the last three days—for this was the object at which Satan aimed. I also confessed my sin of irritability on account of the cold and sought to have my conscience cleansed through the blood of Jesus. He had mercy on me, and my peace was restored. When I returned, I sought the Lord again in prayer and had uninterrupted communion with Him.

July 12. The funds are now reduced to about twenty pounds. But thanks to the Lord, my faith is stronger than it was when we had a larger sum on hand. God has never at any time, from the beginning of the work, allowed me to distrust Him. Nevertheless, real faith is manifested by prayer. Therefore, I prayed with the headmaster of the Boy's Orphan House. Besides my wife and brother Craik, he is the only person I speak to about our financial status.

While we were praying, an orphan child from Frome was brought to us. Some believers sent five pounds with the child. Thus we received a timely answer to our need. We have given permission for seven children to come in and plan to allow five more. Although our funds are low, we trust that God will meet our needs.

July 17 and 18. These two days we have had two special prayer meetings, from six to nine in the evening, to publicly commend the Boy's Orphan House to the Lord. Our funds are now very low. About twenty pounds remain, and in a few days thirty pounds, at least, will be needed. But I *purposely* avoided saying anything about our present needs and only praised God and spoke about the abundance with which our gracious Father, "the Father of the fatherless," has supplied us. The hand of God will be clearly seen when He sends help.

July 22. I walked through our little garden, meditating on Hebrews 13:8, "Jesus Christ the same yesterday, and to day, and for ever." I meditated on His unchangeable love, power, and wisdom while I prayed about my present spiritual and temporal circumstances.

Suddenly, the present need of the Orphan Houses was brought to my mind. I said to myself, "Jesus in His love and power has supplied me with what I have needed for the orphans. In the same unchangeable love and power, He will provide me with what I need for the future." Joy flooded my soul when I realized the unchangeableness of our mighty Lord. About one minute later, a letter arrived with twenty pounds enclosed.

August 29. Sixteen believers were baptized. Among those who were baptized was a brother eighty-four years old and another over seventy. For the latter, his believing wife had prayed thirty-eight years. At last the Lord answered her prayers for his conversion.

August 31. I have been waiting on the Lord for finances because the expense reports from the Girl's Orphan House have arrived, and there is no money available to pay for housekeeping. But the Lord has not yet sent help. When the matron called today for money, one of the laborers gave her two pounds of his own.

September 1. The Lord in His wisdom and love has not yet sent help. Where it comes from is not my concern. But I believe God will, in due time, send help. His hour is not yet come. This is the most trying time that I have had in the ministry concerning finances. But I know that I will yet praise the Lord for His help.

September 5. Our hour of trial continues. The Lord mercifully has given enough to supply our daily necessities. But He gives *by the day* now, and almost *by the hour,* as we need it. Nothing came in yesterday. I sought the Lord again and again, both yesterday and today, and it seems that He is saying, "My hour is not yet come."

I have faith in God. I believe that He will surely send help. Many pounds are needed within a few days, and there is not a penny in hand. This morning two pounds were given for the present needs by one of the laborers in the work.

Evening. The Lord sent help to encourage me to continue to wait on Him and to trust in Him. As I was praying this afternoon, I felt fully assured that the Lord would send help. I praised Him before I saw the answer and asked Him to encourage our hearts, especially that He would not allow my faith to fail.

A few minutes after I had prayed, the headmaster brought more than four pounds which had come in by several small donations. Tomorrow the account books will be brought from the Infant Orphan House, and money must be advanced for housekeeping. I thought for a moment it might be a good idea to keep three pounds of this money for that purpose. But it occurred to me immediately, "Sufficient unto the day is the evil thereof" (Matthew 6:34). The Lord can provide by tomorrow much more than I need; and I, therefore, sent three pounds to one of the sisters whose quarterly salary was due. The remainder went to the Boy's Orphan House for housekeeping. Thus I am still penniless. My hope is in God, and He will provide.

September 6. The account books were brought from the Infant Orphan House, and the matron asked when money would be advanced for housekeeping. I said, "Tomorrow," although I did not have a single penny in hand. About an hour later, the headmaster sent me a note saying that he had received one pound this morning and that last evening another brother sent twenty-nine pounds of salt, forty-four dozen onions, and twenty-six pounds of grain.

September 7. The time had come to send money to the Infant Orphan House, but the Lord had not sent any more. I gave the pound which had come in yesterday and two shillings and twopence which had been put into the box in my house, trusting the good Lord to send in more.

September 8. My gracious Lord has not sent me help yet. Yesterday and today I have been pleading with God, giving reasons why He would be pleased to send help. The arguments which I used are:

1. I began the work for the glory of God that there might be visible proof of God supplying, in answer to prayer only, the necessities of the orphans. He is the living God and eager to answer prayer.

2. God is the "Father of the fatherless," and as their Father, He should be pleased to provide. (See Psalm 68:5.)

3. I have received the children in the name of Jesus. Therefore, He, in these children, has been received, fed, and clothed. (See Mark 9:36-37.)

4. The faith of many of the children of God has been strengthened by this work. If God withheld the means for the future, those who are weak in faith would be discouraged. If the ministry was continued, their faith might still further be strengthened.

5. Many enemies would laugh if the Lord withheld supplies and say, "We knew that this enthusiasm would come to nothing."

6. Many of the children of God, who are uninstructed or in a carnal state, would feel justified to continue their alliance with the world in their ministries. They would continue in their unscrip-

tural proceedings to raise money if He did not help me.

7. God knows that I cannot provide for these children in my own strength. Therefore, He would not allow this burden to lie on me long without sending help.

8. My fellow-laborers in the ministry also trust in Him.

9. I would have to dismiss the children from under our scriptural instruction to their former companions if He does not help me.

10. He could prove wrong those who said, "In the beginning supplies might be expected while the ministry is new, but after a while, people will lose interest and stop supporting it."

11. If He did not provide, how could I explain the many remarkable answers to prayer which He had given to me previously which have shown me that this work is of God?

In some small measure I now understand the meaning of that word, "how long," which frequently occurs in the prayers of the Psalms. But even now, by the grace of God, my eyes are on Him only, and I believe that He will send help.

September 10. Monday morning. No money came in either Saturday or yesterday. The matter has now become a solemn crisis. We called the brothers and sisters together for prayer, and I explained our situation. Despite this trial of faith, I still believe God will help us. Nothing should be purchased that we cannot pay for, and the children should never lack nourishing food and warm clothing. We discussed what unnecessary possessions could be sold.

A few hours later, nine sixpence were anonymously put into the box at Gideon Chapel. This money seemed like a promise that God would have compassion and send more. About ten o'clock, while I was again in prayer for help, a sister gave two sovereigns to my wife for the orphans. She felt she had already delayed too long. A few minutes later, she gave me two sovereigns more. She did all this without knowing anything about our need. Thus the Lord most mercifully has sent us a little help and greatly encouraged my faith.

September 12. The trial still continues. Only nine shillings came in today, given by one of the laborers. In the midst of this great trial of faith, the Lord mercifully keeps me in great peace. He also allows me to see that our labor is not in vain. Yesterday one of the orphans died who was only about nine years old. She had come to know Jesus several months before her death.

September 13. No help has come yet. This morning I told the brothers and sisters about the state of the funds. We prayed together and had a very happy meeting. One of the sisters told me not to trouble myself about her salary because she did not want any for a year.

September 14. I met again with the brothers and sisters for prayer because the Lord has not sent help. After prayer one of the laborers gave me all the money he had, sixteen shillings, saying that it would not be right to pray if he did not give what he had.

Up to this day, the matrons of the three houses had been in the habit of paying the bakers and the milkman weekly. Sometimes we paid the butcher and grocer this way, too. But now, since the Lord provides for us by the day, we consider it wrong to go on any longer in this way, as the week's payment might come due, and we would have no money to meet it.

We want to act according to the commandment of the Lord, "Owe no man any thing" (Romans 13:8). Since the Lord gives us our supplies daily, we purpose to pay for every article when it is purchased. We will never buy anything unless we can pay for it at once, however much it may seem to be needed.

September 15. We met again this morning for prayer. God comforts our hearts, and we are looking for His help. Enough provisions remain for today and tomorrow, but there is no money on hand to buy bread. During the day enough money came in, and we were able to buy the usual quantity of bread and have some money left. May God be praised, who gave us grace to decide not to buy anything for which we cannot pay at once! We thankfully took this money out of our Father's hands as proof that He still cares for us. In His own time, He will send us larger sums.

Chapter 11

TRUSTING GOD FOR EVERY NEED

September 16, 1838. Lord's day afternoon. We met again to pray for supplies for the orphans. We are at peace, and our hope is in God. He will help us although only one shilling has come in since last evening.

September 17. The trial continues. It is now more trying to our faith each day, but I am sure God will send help, if we wait. Several people gave us a few shillings which enabled us to pay the current expenses and to purchase provisions so that nothing in any way has been lacking.

My faith was tried because of the long delay of larger sums coming. When I went to the Scriptures for comfort, my soul was greatly refreshed by Psalm 39. I went cheerfully to meet with my dear fellow-laborers for prayer, read them the Psalm, and encourage them with the precious promises contained in it.

September 18. We received one pound eight shillings to buy the meat and bread which was needed, a little tea for one of the houses, and milk for all—no more than this is needed. Thus the Lord has provided not only for this day, but there is money for bread for the next two days. Now, however, we are in dire straits again. The funds are exhausted. The laborers who had a little money have given their last shillings.

Now observe how the Lord helped us! A lady from London brought a parcel with money and rented a room next door to the Boys' Orphan House. This afternoon she brought me the money which amounted to three pounds two shillings and sixpence. We were at the point of selling these things which could be spared, but this morning I asked the Lord to provide for us in another way.

The money had been near the Orphan Houses for several days without being given. That proved to me that it was in the heart of God from the beginning to help us. But because He delights in the prayers of His children, He allowed us to pray so long. Our tried faith made the answer much sweeter.

I burst into loud praise and thanks the first moment I was alone. I met with my fellow-laborers again this evening for prayer and praise, and their hearts were greatly cheered. This money will easily provide for all that will be needed tomorrow.

September 22. Both yesterday and today we have assembled for prayer and praise. We are in no

101

immediate need, but on the 29th, the rent of the three Orphan Houses will be due. My comfort is in the living God. During this week He helped me in such a remarkable way that it would have been doubly sinful not to have trusted in Him for help under this fresh difficulty. No money came in this morning. About two, the usual time when the teachers are paid, a sovereign was given which partially paid the weekly teacher's salaries. I found that the headmaster had received a sovereign in the morning. By this sovereign, together with the one I had received *just at the moment when it was needed,* we were helped through this day.

September 25. We still meet for daily prayer. In four days the rent for the Orphan Houses will be due, and we have nothing for it. Also the housekeeping money in the three houses is gone again. May the Lord have compassion on us and continue to help us!

September 29. Prayer has been made for several days concerning the rent which is due today. I have been expecting the money, although I did not know where a shilling was to come from. This morning the headmaster called on me, and we prayed together from ten until a quarter to twelve. Twelve o'clock struck, the time when the rent should have been paid, but no money had been sent. For some days I have repeatedly had a misgiving, whether the Lord might not answer us, in order that we would begin to set money aside daily for the rent.

This is only the second complete failure of answer to prayer in the ministry during the past four years and six months. The first was about the half-yearly rent of Castle-Green classrooms due July 1, 1837, which had come in only in part by that time. I am now fully convinced that the rent should be put aside daily or weekly as God prospers us, in order that the work, even in this point, may be a testimony. May the Lord help us to act accordingly, and may He mercifully send in the money to pay the rent!

October 2. The Lord has dealt most bountifully with us during the last three days! Five pounds came in for the orphans. Oh, how kind is the Lord! Yesterday, more came in and defrayed the house-keeping expenses. The Lord also helped me to pay the rent.

October 9. Today we were brought lower than ever. The money for milk in one of the houses was provided by a laborer selling one of his books. The matrons in the Boys' Orphan House had two shillings left this morning. We were wondering whether to buy bread with it or more meat for dinner when the baker left seventy-five loaves of bread as a gift.

October 10. The coal in the Infant Orphan House is gone, and there is little more in the other two houses. Also, the medicine is nearly all gone. We have asked the Lord for fresh supplies.

October 11. The "Father of the fatherless" has again shown His care for us. An orphan from Devonshire arrived last evening. With her was sent some money and silver articles that we sold for sixteen pounds. Thus we were helped through the heavy expenses of the following days.

October 12. Seven brothers and sisters were added to us in fellowship. May the Lord send helpers for the work!

October 15. I knew that money would be needed this morning for many things in the Orphan Houses, and my heart was therefore lifted up in prayer to the Lord. Just when I was going to meet my fellow-laborers for prayer, several pounds arrived. We were able to purchase medicine and a ton of coal. Now, however, we must depend on the love of our Lord for further supplies because there is nothing in hand, and the laborers do not have any more of their own to give.

October 29. The Lord has again given us this day our daily bread, although in the morning there was not the least prospect of obtaining supplies. We are trusting in God day by day. He meets our needs faithfully in so many ways as we wait patiently upon Him. Our needs are great, but His help is also great.

November 10. All seemed to be dark at the beginning of this day. But the Lord has enabled us to meet all financial demands. One more week has ended, and we have been able to supply the needs of ninety-seven people in the Orphan Houses, without going into debt.

November 21. Not even a single halfpenny was left in the three houses. Nevertheless, we had a good dinner, and by sharing our bread, we made it through this day also. When I left the brothers and sisters after prayer, I told them we must wait for help and see how the Lord would deliver us this time. I was sure of help, but we were indeed in another serious situation.

When I left the meeting, I felt that I needed more exercise so I walked home a longer way. About twenty yards from my house, I met a brother who walked back with me. After a little conversation, he gave me ten pounds to provide the poor saints with coal, blankets, and warm clothing. He also gave five pounds for the orphans and five pounds for the other needs of the Scriptural Knowledge Institution. The brother had come to see me twice while I was away at the Orphan House. Had I been *one half minute later,* I would have missed him. But the Lord knew our need, and therefore allowed me to meet him.

November 24. This has been a very remarkable day. We had little money in hand this morning, and several pounds were needed. But God, who is rich in mercy and whose Word positively declares that none who trust in Him will be disappointed, has helped us through this day also. While I was in prayer about the funds, I was informed that a gentleman had called to see me. He informed me that a lady ordered three sacks of potatoes to be sent to the Orphan Houses. They could not have come at a better time! This was an encouragement to me to continue to expect help.

November 28. This is perhaps the most remarkable day as yet! When I was in prayer this morning, I firmly believed that the Lord would send help, although all seemed dark to natural appearances. At twelve o'clock I met as usual with the brothers and sisters for prayer. Only one shilling had come in, and all but twopence had already been spent. I found that we had everything necessary for the dinner in the three houses, but neither in the Infant's nor in the Boys' Orphan House was there enough bread for tea or money to buy milk. We united in prayer, leaving the situation in the hands of the Lord.

While we prayed, there was a knock at the door, and one of the sisters went out. After the two brethren and I had prayed aloud, we continued for a while silently in prayer. I was lifting up my heart to the Lord, asking Him to make a way for our escape. I asked Him if there was any other thing which I could do with a good conscience, besides waiting on Him, so that we might have food for the children.

At last we rose from our knees. I said, "God will surely send help." The words had not quite passed over my lips when I saw a letter lying on the table, which had been brought while we were in prayer. It contained ten pounds for the orphans.

Last evening a brother asked me whether the money in hand for the orphans would be as large this time, when the accounts would be closed, as it was the last time. My answer was that it would be as great as the Lord pleased. The next morning, this brother was moved to send ten pounds for the orphans which arrived after I had left my house, and which, on account of our need, was forwarded immediately to me. He also sent ten pounds to be divided between Brother Craik and me to purchase new clothes.

November 29. The Lord has greatly blessed our meetings for prayer. We pray much for the children in the Orphan Houses, in the day schools, and in the Sunday school. We also pray for ourselves and for the teachers that grace may be given to us to walk before the children and to deal with them in such a way that the Lord may be glorified. We also intercede for the believers with whom we are in fellowship and for the Church at large. We especially pray that our work may lead the Church to a more simple confidence and trust in the Lord.

These meetings have not been in vain. Larger donations of fifty and one hundred pounds came in. One sister told us that she gave in obedience to scriptural exhortations—"Having food and raiment let us be therewith content" (1 Timothy 6:8). "Sell that ye have, and give alms; provide yourselves bags which wax not old, a treasure in the heavens that faileth not, where no thief approacheth, neither moth corrupteth" (Luke

12:33). "Lay not up for yourselves treasures upon earth, where moth and rust doth corrupt, and where thieves break through and steal: But lay up for yourselves treasures in heaven, where neither moth nor rust doth corrupt, and where thieves do not break through nor steal" (Matthew 6:19-20).

Fifty pounds have been given for the school, Bible, and missionary fund. We would not order more Bibles until we had the means to pay for them. We repeatedly prayed concerning this need for Bibles. We also asked God to supply us abundantly, if it was His will, that at the public meetings we might be able to speak again of God's gracious provision. Otherwise, it might appear that we had scheduled the meeting for the sake of telling people about our poverty, and thus induce them to give.

December 11, 12, and 13. On the evenings of these last three days, we held public meetings. I gave an account of the Lord's dealing with us in the Orphan Houses and the Scriptural Knowledge Institution. Because the work, particularly that of the Orphan Houses, was begun for the benefit of the Church at large, we believed that from time to time it should be publicly stated how the Lord has dealt with us. On December 9, the third year was completed since the beginning of the orphan ministry. Therefore, this seemed to be a suitable time for having these meetings.

Presently a Sunday school is supported by the Scriptural Knowledge Institution which teaches

463 children. This part of the work calls for particular thanksgiving. During these last eighteen months, the number of the children is nearly three times as great as it used to be. Five of the scholars have been converted within the last two years and are now in fellowship with the church. Three of them are now teachers in the school.

Over 120 adults have been instructed, and twelve have been taught to read. The Institution entirely supported several day schools for poor children—three for boys and three for girls. The number of all the children that have had schooling in the day schools through the Institution is 1,534. In the six schools, we have 342 children.

During the last two years we circulated 1,884 copies of the Scriptures in connection with the Institution, and since the beginning of the work, 5,078 copies. Missionary work has been supported also.

Eighty-six orphans live in the three houses. The number of orphans who have been under our care from April 11, 1836, to December 9, 1838, amounts to 110.

December 16. A paper was anonymously placed into the box at Bethesda Chapel containing four pounds ten shillings. In the paper was written, "For the rent of the Orphan Houses from December 10 to December 31, 1838."

"O taste and see that the Lord is good: blessed is the man that trusteth in him!" (Psalm 34:8). The individual who gave this four pounds ten shillings for the rent of the Orphan Houses decided to give regularly, but anonymously, one pound ten shillings every week which was exactly the sum required for the rent of those three houses. Thus the Lord rewarded our obedience.

December 20. The expenses for the orphans have been more than forty-seven pounds within the last six days, and only a little above thirteen pounds has come in. We are again very low in funds.

I gave myself this morning to prayer. About a quarter of an hour afterward I received three pounds, the payment of a will left by a sister who died several months ago.

December 22. A solemn day. I received word that my brother died on October 7. "Shall not the Judge of all the earth do right?" (Genesis 18:25). This must be the comfort to the believer at such a time, and it is my comfort now. I know that the Lord is glorified in my brother, whatever his end has been. May the Lord make this event a lasting blessing to me, especially in leading me to earnest prayer for my father!

December 31. We have had many expenses during the past year, but during no period of my life has the Lord so richly supplied me. Truly, it must be obvious to all that I serve a kind Master. It is by far best to act according to the will of the Lord concerning temporal things!

Chapter 12

ASKING AND RECEIVING

January 1, 2, and 3, 1839. We have had three special prayer meetings these three days. The year began with blessings. In the first hour of the year, two pounds seven shillings came in for the orphans. The money was given after our usual prayer meeting on December 31, which lasted from seven in the evening until after midnight.

January 20. "Ye have the poor with you always, and whensoever ye will ye may do them good" (Mark 14:7). The Lord spoke these words to His disciples, who were themselves very poor, implying that the children of God have power with God to bring temporal blessings upon poor saints or poor unbelievers through prayer. Accordingly, I have been led to ask the Lord for means to assist poor saints, and He has stirred His children to trust me with money for that purpose.

Therefore, I had been praying again for means to more extensively assist the poor saints in communion with us. Many of them are not merely tried by the usual temporal difficulties arising from winter, but especially from the high price of bread. This evening the Lord has given me the answer to my prayer. When I came home from the meeting, I found a brother at my house who offered to give me ten pounds a week for twelve weeks to provide the poor saints with coal, clothing, and bread.

February 7. This day has been one of the most remarkable days concerning the funds. There was no money on hand, and I was waiting on God. I asked Him repeatedly, but no supplies came. The headmaster called to tell me that one pound two shillings was needed to buy bread for the three houses and to meet the other expenses. He then left for Clifton to make arrangements to receive the three orphans of a sister who passed away on the 4th. Although we have no funds on hand, the work goes on, and our confidence is not diminished. I requested him to call, on his way back from Clifton, to see whether the Lord had sent any money in the meantime. When he returned, I had received nothing, but one of the laborers gave five shillings of his own.

At four o'clock I wondered how the sisters had gotten through the day. I went to the Girls' Orphan House to meet for prayer and found that a box had come for me from Barnstable. The delivery fee was paid, otherwise there would have been no money to pay for it. See how the Lord's hand is in the smallest matters! The box was opened, and it contained more than fourteen pounds for the orphans and for the Bible Fund. Besides this, there were four yards of cloth, three pairs of new shoes, two pairs of new socks, six books for sale, a gold pencil-case, two gold rings, two gold earrings, a necklace, and a silver pencil-case.

March 5. Several pounds were needed again. Besides the daily provisions, the coal was low, the medical supplies in two houses were exhausted, and there were only five shillings in hand. While I was in prayer this morning, I received a check for seven pounds ten shillings.

March 23. By means of several donations I am able both to meet the remaining expenses of this week and also to pay fifteen pounds which still remain due for the salaries. My fellow-laborers never ask me for anything and are willing to part with money or anything else in the hour of need. Nevertheless, I asked the Lord about this frequently, and He has now granted my request.

April 13. I conversed with another of the orphans who has walked consistently with the Lord for many months. Tomorrow she will be united with the saints in communion.

April 14. A poor brother with a large family and small wages saved the money given to him by his boss for beer. This brother, who was converted about five years ago, used to be a notorious drunkard. When the money accumulated to one pound, he donated it to the orphans.

July 15. Two pounds seven shillings was needed for the orphans, but we had nothing. I had no idea how to obtain the means for dinner and for our other needs. My heart was perfectly at peace and sure of help. That afternoon I received a letter from India, written in May, with fifty pounds for the orphans. I had said last Saturday that we could use fifty pounds because the salaries of all my fellow-laborers are due, medical supplies are gone, provisions are exhausted, articles of clothing are needed, and wool yarn is needed for the boys to go on with their knitting.

August 22. In my morning walk, when I was reminding the Lord of our need, I felt assured that He would send help this day. My assurance sprang from our need, for there seemed no way to get through the day without help being sent. After breakfast I considered what might be sold for money for the dear children. But all seemed not nearly enough to meet the requirements of the day.

In our deep poverty, after I had gathered together a few things for sale, a sister who earns her living by the labor of her hands brought eighty-two pounds. This sister was convinced that believers in our Lord Jesus should act out His commandments: "Sell that ye have, and give alms" (Luke 12:33); "Lay not up for yourselves treasures upon earth" (Matthew 6:19). Accordingly, she drew her money out of the bank and stocks, two hundred and fifty pounds, and brought it to me at three different times for the benefit of the orphans, the Bible, missionary, and school funds, and the poor saints.

About two months ago she brought me one hundred pounds more after she had sold some other possessions. The eighty-two pounds she brought today is from the sale of her last earthly possession. She never expressed the least regret for the step she took, but went on quietly laboring with her hands to earn her daily living.

September 4. I have been led to pray whether it is the Lord's will that I leave Bristol for a season. For the last two weeks I have suffered from severe indigestion, and my whole system is weakened. Two hindrances stand in the way—lack of money for the orphans and for my own personal expenses. Today I received a check for seven pounds ten shillings for the orphans, which came at an excellent time. Also four pounds have come in since the day before yesterday.

September 5. Today a sister sent me five pounds for myself, to be used for the benefit of my health which she had heard is again failing. I do not put aside money for such purposes; but whenever I really need means, whether for myself or others, the Lord sends it in answer to prayer.

September 7. I arrived in Trowbridge. This has been a very good day. I had much communion with the Lord. How kind He is to take me from the work in Bristol for a season and give me more communion with Himself. I remembered the Lord's special blessing on me in this place at the beginning of last year. How kind He has been since! I prayed much for myself, for the Church at large, for the saints here and in Bristol, for my unconverted relatives, for my dear wife, and that the Lord would supply my own temporal necessities and those of the orphans. I know that He has heard me.

I am surrounded with kind friends, and I feel quite at home. My room is far better than I need, but an easy chair to kneel before in prayer would add to my comfort since my body is so weak. In the afternoon, without me making a hint about it, I found that someone had placed an easy chair into my room. I was amazed by the special kindness of my heavenly Father. He is mindful of the smallest wants and comforts of His child.

September 9. I returned to Bristol and to my old habit of rising early in the morning to commune with God. I was led to it by the example of the brother in whose house I was staying. He remarked when speaking on the sacrifices in Leviticus that, just as only the best animals were to be offered up, the best part of our time should be given to communion with the Lord.

I had been an early riser in the past. But since my nerves became so weak, I thought it best for me to have more rest. For this reason I rose between six and seven, and sometimes after seven. I purposely got into the habit of sleeping a quarter of an hour or half an hour after dinner.

I thought I found benefit from the much-needed

relaxation. In this way, however, my soul had suffered considerably. Unavoidable work often came upon me before I had sufficient time for prayer and reading the Word.

I finally decided that, whatever my body might suffer, I would no longer let the most precious part of the day pass away while I was in bed. By the grace of God I was able to begin the very next day to rise earlier and have continued to rise early since that time. I allow myself now about seven hours of sleep. Although I am far from being strong and have much to tire me mentally, I find this is quite sufficient to refresh me. In addition, I gave up sleeping after dinner. The result has been that I can have long and precious times for prayer and meditation before breakfast.

Concerning my body and the state of my nerves, I have been much better since. The worst thing I could have done for my weak nerves was to have lain an hour or more in bed than I used to before my illness because it actually weakened my body.

I want to encourage all believers to get into the habit of rising early to meet with God. How much time should be allowed for rest? No rule of universal application can be given because all persons do not require the same amount of sleep. Also the same persons, at different times, according to the strength or weakness of their body, may require more or less. Most doctors agree that healthy men do not require more than between six or seven hours of sleep, and females need no more than seven or eight hours.

Children of God should be careful not to allow themselves too little sleep since few men can do with less than six hours of sleep and still be well in body and mind. As a young man, before I went to the university, I went to bed regularly at ten and rose at four, studied hard, and was in good health. Since I have allowed myself only about seven hours, I have been much better in body and in nerves than when I spent eight or eight and a half hours in bed.

Someone may ask, "But why should I rise early?" To remain too long in bed is a waste of time. Wasting time is unbecoming a saint who is bought by the precious blood of Jesus. His time and all he has is to be used for the Lord. If we sleep more than is necessary for the refreshment of the body, it is wasting the time the Lord has entrusted us to be used for His glory, for our own benefit, and for the benefit of the saints and unbelievers around us.

Just as too much food injures the body, the same is true regarding sleep. Medical persons would readily agree that lying longer in bed than is necessary to strengthen the body actually weakens it.

It also injures the soul. Lying too long in bed not merely keeps us from giving the most precious part of the day to prayer and meditation, but this sloth leads also to many other evils. Anyone who spends one, two, or three hours in prayer and meditation before breakfast will soon discover the beneficial effect early rising has on the outward and inward man.

It may be said, "But how shall I set about rising early?" My advice is: Do not delay. Begin tomorrow. But do not depend on your own strength. You may have begun to rise early in the past but have given it up. If you depend on your own strength in this matter, it will come to nothing. In every good work, we must depend on the Lord. If anyone rises so that he may give the time which he takes from sleep to prayer and meditation, let him be sure that Satan will try to put obstacles in the way.

Trust in the Lord for help. You will honor Him if you expect help from Him in this matter. Pray for help, expect help, and you will have it. In addition to this, go to bed early. If you stay up late, you cannot rise early. Let no pressure of engagements keep you from going habitually early to bed. If you fail in this, you neither can nor should get up early because your body requires rest.

Rise at once when you are awake. Remain not a minute longer in bed or else you are likely to fall asleep again. Do not be discouraged by feeling drowsy and tired from rising early. This will soon wear off. After a few days you will feel stronger and fresher than when you used to lie an hour or two longer than you needed. Always allow yourself the same hours for sleep. Make no change except on account of sickness.

On December 10, 11, and 12 we had public meetings at which the account of the Lord's dealings with us in the Orphan Houses and the Scriptural Knowledge Institution was given. It is now five years and nine months since the Scriptural Knowledge Institution has been in operation. We have been able to continue to provide for all the necessary expenses connected with the six day schools. The number of children in them is 286. The number of all the children that have had schooling in the day schools amounts to 1,795.

There are 226 children in the Sunday school. Fourteen are being taught to read in the adult school, and there have been about 130 adults instructed in that school since the formation of the Institution.

We have circulated, during the last year, 514 copies of the Scriptures and 5,592 since March 5, 1834. Missionary work has also been supported.

There are now 96 orphans in the three houses. The number of all the orphans who have been under our care from April 11, 1836, to December 9, 1839, amounts to 126. Everything has been given to us entirely as the result of prayer to God.

Chapter 13

LOOKING TO THE LORD

January 1, 1840. About one o'clock this morning, I received a sealed envelope with some money in it for the orphans. The individual who gave it was deeply in debt, and I was aware that she had been repeatedly asked by her creditors for payment. I resolved to return the envelope without opening it because no one has a right to give while in debt. I did this although I knew there was not enough on hand to meet the expenses of the day. About eight o'clock this morning a brother brought five pounds which he had just received from his mother. The brother was led to bring it *at once!*

January 25. I have prayed much this week about going to Germany to see certain brothers who plan to go as missionaries to the East Indies and to see my father once more. I am led to go just now, instead of delaying the trip, because my health is again failing. This way, I will continue to serve in the work of the Lord and benefit my health at the same time. Lord, keep me from making a mistake in this matter!

February 2. Today and yesterday nearly nine pounds have come in for the orphans. How kind of the Lord to send this money on the eve of my leaving home!

March 9. During my absence from Bristol, the Lord not only supplied all the needs of the orphans, but when I returned, He supplied even more than there was when I left.

March 26. On the 17th of this month I received the following letter from a brother who had been used by the Lord several times to supply our need.

"I have received a little money. Do you have any present need for the institution under your care? I know you do not *ask,* except of Him whose work you are doing; but to answer when asked seems to be a right thing to do. I have a reason for desiring to know the present state of your finances. If you do not need the money, other areas of the Lord's work or other people of the Lord may need help. Kindly inform me the amount you need at this present time."

When this letter came, we were in need. Nevertheless, I answered it as follows:

"While I thank you for your love, and while I agree with you that there is a difference between *asking for money* and *answering when asked,* nevertheless, I do not feel at liberty to speak about the state of our funds. The primary object of this ministry is to lead those who are weak in faith to see that there is *reality* in dealing with God *alone."*

After I sent off the answer, I prayed, "Lord, You know that for Your sake I did not tell this brother about our need. Now, Lord, show afresh that there is reality in speaking to You only about our need. Speak to this brother, so that he may help us."

Today, in answer to my request, this brother sent one hundred pounds. I now have money for establishing the infant school and for ordering more Bibles. Also, the orphans are again supplied for a week.

April 7. This evening I received information that my dear father died on March 30. During no period did I pray more frequently or more earnestly for his conversion than during the last year of his life. But I did not *see* the answer to my prayers.

May 2. Nothing has come in for five days, and we are penniless again. In answer to prayer, five shillings sixpence came in, and some trinkets were sent. Thus we were helped through this day. The Lord allowed five days to pass away without influencing the hearts of any to send us supplies, but the moment there is real need, the stream runs again.

May 3. Last evening a brother was baptized, who on the first Sunday of this year came with his fiancee to Bethesda Chapel. Neither were believers at the time. Since April 1, forty-one people have come to us to speak about their souls.

May 10. Today five of the orphans were baptized. There are now fourteen of them in fellowship.

May 26. Nothing had come in. My other work kept me from going to the Orphan Houses until seven in the evening when the workers met together for prayer. One of them had given seventeen shillings which had been divided between the three houses. With this we purchased all necessary articles. We are now very poor.

May 27. We met for prayer at eleven this morning. No money had come in, but there was enough for dinner in all the houses. This morning the last of the coal was used in the Infant Orphan House. In the Boys'. Orphan House was enough coal for today but no money to buy more. In our time of need, a brother sent a load of coal. We plan to meet this afternoon for more prayer. May the Lord graciously send help in the meantime!

Evening. The Lord has had mercy! Several days ago a person gave us several articles to be sold for the benefit of the orphans. He owed us six pounds fifteen shillings. This morning I asked the Lord to incline his heart to bring the money, or at least a part of it, since we were in such need. Just as I was going to meet for prayer with my fellow-laborers this afternoon, he brought four pounds.

But our kind Father showed us further that He had withheld supplies for a season only to test our faith. Enough has come in to supply us for several days. Thus the day, which had begun with prayer, ended in praise. But I must mention one more thing which is even more precious: the Lord has begun to work in the hearts of several of the boys. They want to learn more about Jesus.

August 1. A few days ago a brother was staying with me. He was on his way to visit his father whom he had not seen for more than two years. His father was greatly opposed to the decided steps his son had taken to serve the Lord. Before this brother left, that precious promise of our Lord was brought to my mind: "If two of you shall agree on earth as touching any thing that they shall ask, it shall be done for them of my Father which is in heaven" (Matthew 18:19). Accordingly, I went to the brother's room, and we prayed together for a kind reception from his father and the conversion of both parents.

Today this brother returned. The Lord has already answered one part of the prayer—he was kindly received, contrary to all natural expectation. May the Lord now help us both to look for an answer to the other part of our prayer! Nothing is too hard for the Lord!

[The father of this brother lived ten more years after August 1, 1840, until he was about eighty-six years of age. He continued in a life of much sin and opposition to the truth, and the prospect of his conversion became darker and darker. But at last the Lord answered prayer. This aged sinner was entirely changed, trusted in the Lord Jesus for the salvation of his soul, and became as much attached to his believing son as before he had been opposed to him. He wanted his son near him as much as possible to read the Holy Scriptures to him and pray with him.]

August 8. This evening I was meditating on the fourth Psalm. The words in verse three, "But know that the Lord hath set apart him that is godly for himself: the Lord will hear when I call unto him," spoke to my heart and led me to pray for spiritual blessings. While in prayer, the needs of the orphans were brought to my mind, and I prayed about this, too.

About five minutes later, I was informed that a sister wished to see me. She brought one pound ten shillings for the orphans. Thus the Lord has already kindly sent a little to begin the week with.

August 23. As we have often found it to be the case, so it is again now. After the Lord has tried our faith, He, in the love of His heart, gives us an abundance. For the glory of His name and for the trial of our faith, He allows us to be poor and then graciously supplies our needs.

August 29. Very little has come in for the other funds. The chief supply of our needs has been by the sale of Bibles. Last Saturday I was not able to pay all of the weekly salaries of the teachers in the day schools. However, I am not a debtor to them because it is understood that they must not look to me for payment, but to the Lord. It appeared now to be the will of the Lord that the brothers and sisters who labor in the day schools would also share the trials and joys of living by faith with us. We all met, and after I had laid on their hearts the importance of keeping the state of funds to themselves, we prayed together.

September 5. Because so little has come in during the last days, at least three pounds was required to supply the needs of today. Not one penny, however, was in hand when the day began. In the afternoon, all of us met for prayer. A few teachers gave some of their own money, but it was not enough. Dinner has not been provided for tomorrow and there is no money to buy milk.

Now observe how our kind Father helped us! This evening a sister who sells some things for us brought two pounds ten shillings sixpence. Though she did not feel well, she said she had come because it was on her heart, and she could not stay away.

September 8. Our prayer meetings have been a blessing to us and united us more than ever in the work. We have them now every morning at seven; and we will continue them, the Lord helping us, until we see His hand stretched forth. We need a stove in one of the schoolrooms and a supply of Bibles and New Testaments. We also want to help missionary brethren who labor in dependence upon the Lord for the supply of their temporal necessities.

September 21. A brother from London gave me ten pounds to be used where it was needed most. This brother knew nothing about our work when he came to Bristol three days ago. The Lord shows us His continual care over us by raising up new helpers.

Those who trust in the Lord will never be disappointed. Some who helped us for a while may fall asleep in Jesus, some may grow cold in the service of the Lord, some may be as desirous as ever to help but no longer have the means, and some may have both a willing heart to help and the means but may see it to be the Lord's will to give in another way. If we were to lean upon man, we would surely be disappointed; but in leaning upon the living God alone, we are beyond disappointment and beyond being forsaken for any reason.

October 7. It is now five weeks since we met daily for prayer. In addition to temporal needs, we ask for grace and wisdom for ourselves in the work, for the conversion of the children under our care, for grace for those children who have already accepted the Lord, for a blessing upon the distribution of the Scriptures, and for a blessing upon the work of the Church at large.

Never since the work began have we had to continue so long in prayer for funds without obtaining the answer. The Lord, however, gave us grace to continue in prayer, and He kept our hearts in the assurance that He would help. Now, in His own time, He made it manifest that He had not only heard our prayers, but that He had answered them *even before we called*. Today we received from the East Indies a bank order for one hundred pounds, which had been sent two months ago—several days before we even began to pray.

November 8. I planned to go to Trowbridge yesterday and had made the arrangements on Friday evening. But no sooner had I decided to do so, than I felt no peace about going. After praying about it on Friday evening and yesterday morning, I decided not to go. I began to look for blessings for this day, believing that the Lord had kept me here for a good reason.

This evening I was led to share the truth of the gospel with some who had not yet accepted Jesus as their Lord. I immediately saw fruit from the Word. I talked with one man until about ten o'clock, as long as I had any strength left. The Lord, in His mercy toward them, kept me from going to Trowbridge.

December 9. Although our trials of faith during this year have been more than during any previous year, and although we have been often reduced to the greatest extremity, yet the orphans have lacked nothing. They always have had good nourishing food and the necessary articles of clothing.

If anyone thinks that on account of our trials of faith during this year we have been disappointed in our expectations or discouraged in the work, my answer is that the very opposite is true. Such days were expected from the beginning. The chief end for which the institution was established is that the Church would see the hand of God stretched out on our behalf in answer to prayer.

Our desire, therefore, is not that we may be without trials of faith, but that the Lord would graciously support us in the trial and that we may not dishonor Him by distrust.

This way of living brings the Lord remarkably near. Morning by morning, He inspects our supplies that He may send help as it is needed. I have never had a greater awareness of the Lord's presence than when after breakfast nothing was left for dinner, and then the Lord provided the dinner for more than one hundred people; or when, after dinner, there was nothing for the tea, and yet the Lord provided the tea—all this without one single human being having been informed about our need. One thing is certain—we are not tired of doing the Lord's work in this way.

Many people have commented that such a way of living must cause the mind to continually think of how to obtain food and clothes, and thus become unfit for spiritual work. I answer that our minds are seldom concerned about the necessities of life because the care for them is laid upon our Father. Because we are His children, He not only allows us to do so but wants us to do so.

Do not think that these answers to prayer are only for us and cannot be enjoyed by all the saints. Every child of God is not called by the Lord to establish schools and orphan houses and to trust in the Lord for means for them. Yet, there is no reason why you may not experience, far more abundantly than we do now, His willingness to answer the prayers of His children.

Prove the faithfulness of God by carrying your every want to Him. Only maintain an upright heart. But if you live in sin and if you willfully and habitually do things which you know are contrary to the will of God, then you cannot expect Him to hear you. "If I regard iniquity in my heart, the Lord will not hear me: But verily God hath heard me; he hath attended to the voice of my prayer" (Psalm 66:18-19).

A few more interesting points are:

1. During this year, six day schools for poor children have been entirely supported by the funds of our institution. The number of all the children that have had schooling in the day schools through the institution, since its formation, amounts to 2,216. The number of those at present in the six day schools is 303.

These day schools have been assisted by the children paying about one-sixth of their own expenses.

2. One Sunday school has been entirely supported by the funds of the institution.

3. Since the formation of the institution, one adult school has been connected with it. On Sunday afternoons since it began, about 150 adults have been instructed.

4. We have given out many Bibles and Testaments and supported missionary work.

5. During the last fourteen months, we have

held Bible studies especially for the children. They have shown great interest in these meetings, and I thankfully ascribe this to the Lord. I believe it is a forerunner of greater blessing.

6. During the last year, three of the Sunday school children have been received into fellowship. At the end of last year, eight orphans received communion; and during the present year, fourteen more were received.

In last year's report we stated that we were looking for fruit in the conversion of the children. We have prayed earnestly for them, and the Lord has dealt with us according to our expectations. But I expect far more than what we have seen. The chief object of our work is to demonstrate the reality of power with God in prayer. As we hoped and as it has been our prayer, the Lord gives us the joy of seeing one child after another brought to Him.

It appears to me that believers generally have expected far too little present fruit from their labors among children. They hope that the Lord will some day confirm their instruction and answer the prayers which they offer up on the children's behalf. The Bible assures us that in everything we do for the Lord, including bringing up children in the fear of the Lord, our labor is not in vain. We have to guard against thinking that it does not matter whether we see present fruit or not. On the contrary, we should give the Lord no rest until we see fruit. Therefore, in persevering yet submissive prayer, we should make our requests known to God. I am now looking for many more children to be converted.

Chapter 14

FAITH STRENGTHENED BY EXERCISE

January 1, 1841. During this week we have met daily for prayer, asking the Lord for the means to have last year's report printed. It is three weeks since it should have been sent to the press. If the report is not printed soon, people will know that it is because we lack money.

By the donations which came in during these last days for the orphans, and by ten pounds which was given today, we can pay for about two thirds of the printing. Therefore, we sent a part of the manuscript, trusting that the Lord would send in more money. But if not, we will wait until more comes in.

January 11. During the last week, the Lord not only supplied us richly with all we needed for the orphans, but He enabled us to put several pounds aside for printing the report. On Saturday evening only three shillings were left. I was expecting an answer to my prayers for funds, and the Lord did not disappoint me. More money came yesterday, and we now have enough to print the last part of the report.

January 12. Today I received a letter from a brother who gave me the right to draw upon his bank account during this year, up to one thousand pounds. It may be used for any brother or sister who have it in their hearts to serve as missionaries in the East Indies and whom I consider called for this service, as far as I am able to judge.

[This power lasted only for that year, but no suitable people offered themselves for this service. Finances can be obtained much more easily than suitable individuals. Indeed, in all my experience, I have found that if I could only settle that a certain thing to be done was according to the will of God, the money was soon obtained to carry it into effect.]

March 4. For the encouragement of believers who are tried by having unconverted relatives and friends, I will relate the following circumstance which I know is true. Baron von Kamp, who lived in Prussia, had been a disciple of the Lord Jesus for many years. In the year 1806, great financial distress came upon many thousands of weavers in the area. They had no employment because the whole continent was in an unsettled state from the war. The baron believed that it was the will of the Lord to use his wealth to furnish these poor weavers with work, in order to save them from complete ruin. There was not only no prospect of personal gain, but rather the certain prospect of immense loss. Nevertheless, he found employment for about six thousand weavers.

But the baron was not content with this. He also wanted to minister to the souls of these weavers. He set believers as overseers over his immense weaving concern. The weavers were instructed in spiritual things, and he personally shared the truth of the gospel with them.

The work went on for a good while until at last, on account of the loss of most of his property, he was obliged to think about giving it up. But by this time, his precious act of mercy had proven its worth to the government. It was taken up by them and carried on until the times changed. Baron von Kamp was appointed director of the whole concern as long as it existed.

This dear man of God was not content with this. He traveled through many countries to visit the prisons for the sake of improving the physical and spiritual condition of the prisoners. He also assisted poor students at the university of Berlin, especially those who studied theology, in order to win them for the Lord.

One day a talented young man heard of the aged baron's kindness to students. He wrote to the baron, requesting his assistance because his own father could not afford to support him any longer. A short time afterward, young Thomas received a kind reply from the baron, inviting him to come to Berlin. But before this letter arrived, the young student had heard that Baron von Kamp was a "pietist" or "mystic," as true believers were contemptuously called in Germany. Young Thomas was deeply involved in philosophy, reasoning about everything, questioning the truth of revelation, questioning even the existence of God. He disliked the prospect of going to the old baron for help. Still, he thought he could try, and if he did not like it, he was not obligated to remain in connection with him.

Thomas arrived in Berlin on a day when the baron was out of town on business. He began to speak about his philosophies to the steward of the baron. The steward, however, was a believer, and he turned the conversation to spiritual things.

At last the baron arrived. He received Thomas in the most affectionate and familiar manner. The baron offered him a room in his house and a place at his table while Thomas studied in Berlin. Thomas accepted the offer.

The baron now sought in every way to treat the young student in the most kind and affectionate way, to serve him as much as possible, and to show him the power of the gospel in his own life. He did all this without arguing with him or even speaking to him directly about his soul. Thomas obviously had a skeptical mind, and the baron avoided getting into any argument with him. The student often said to himself, "I wish I could get into an argument with this old fool. I would show him how irrational his beliefs are." But the baron avoided it.

When the baron heard the young student come home in the evening, he would go to meet him and serve him in any way he could, even helping him to take off his boots. Thus this lowly, aged disciple went on for some time. While Thomas still sought an opportunity for arguing with him, he wondered how the baron could continue to serve him.

One evening when Thomas returned to the baron's house, the baron was making himself his servant as usual. The student could restrain himself no longer and burst out, "Baron, how can you do all this? You see I do not care about you. How are you able to continue to be so kind to me and serve me like this?"

The baron replied, "My dear young friend, I have learned it from the Lord Jesus. I wish you would read through the gospel of John. Good night."

The student now for the first time in his life sat down and read the Word of God with an open heart and a willingness to learn. Up to that time, he had never read the Holy Scriptures unless he wanted to find out arguments against them. God blessed him. From that time he became a follower of the Lord Jesus and has continued in the faith ever since.

May 7. The primary business I must attend to every day is to fellowship with the Lord. The first concern is not how much I might serve the Lord, but how my inner man might be nourished. I may share the truth with the unconverted; I may try to encourage believers; I may relieve the distressed; or I may, in other ways, seek to behave as a child of God; yet, not being happy in the Lord and not being nourished and strengthened in my inner man day by day, may result in this work being done in a wrong spirit.

The most important thing I had to do was to read the Word of God and to meditate on it. Thus my heart might be comforted, encouraged, warned, reproved, and instructed.

Formerly, when I rose, I began to pray as soon as possible. But I often spent a quarter of an hour to an hour on my knees struggling to pray while my mind wandered. Now I rarely have this problem. As my heart is nourished by the truth of the Word, I am brought into true fellowship with God. I speak to my Father and to my Friend (although I am unworthy) about the things that He has brought before me in His precious Word.

It often astonishes me that I did not see the importance of meditation upon Scripture earlier in my Christian life. As the outward man is not fit for work for any length of time unless he eats, so it is with the inner man. What is the food for the inner man? Not prayer, but *the Word of God*—not the simple reading of the Word of God, so that it only passes through our minds, just as water runs through a pipe. No, we must consider what we read, ponder over it, and apply it to our hearts.

When we pray, we speak to God. This exercise

of the soul can be best performed after the inner man has been nourished by meditation on the Word of God. Through His Word, our Father speaks to us, encourages us, comforts us, instructs us, humbles us, and reproves us. We may profitably meditate, with God's blessing, although we are spiritually weak. The weaker we are, the more meditation we need to strengthen our inner man. Meditation on God's Word has given me the help and strength to pass peacefully through deep trials. What a difference there is when the soul is refreshed in fellowship with God early in the morning! Without spiritual preparation, the service, the trials, and the temptations of the day can be overwhelming.

October 1. When I had not one penny in hand for the needs of this day, ten shillings were brought to me for the orphans. The enclosed note read: "Your heavenly Father knows that you need these things. Trust in the Lord." This word of our Lord is to me more valuable than many bank notes.

November 2. At the time of our great poverty, one pound was sent by a lady from Birmingham. About half an hour later, I received ten pounds from a brother who had saved up one hundred and fifty pounds. He put it into a savings bank, but he now sees that to devote this money to the work of God glorifies the name of Jesus more than to keep it in the savings bank for a time of sickness or old age. If such times come, the same Lord who has cared for him in health and strength will also care for him then.

In Matthew 6:19-21, it is written: "Lay not up for yourselves treasures upon earth, where moth and rust doth corrupt, and where thieves break through and steal: But lay up for yourselves treasures in heaven, where neither moth nor rust doth corrupt, and where thieves do not break through nor steal: for where your treasure is, there will your heart be also."

The Lord Jesus, our Lord and Master, knows what is best for our true welfare and happiness. His disciples are strangers and pilgrims on earth—we neither belong to the earth nor expect to remain in it. Therefore, we should not seek to increase our earthly possessions.

This is a word for poor believers as well as for rich believers. It may be said, "But every prudent person seeks to increase his wealth that he may have plenty to leave his children or to have something for old age or for the time of sickness." This is the custom of the world. But we disciples of the Lord Jesus have been promised "an inheritance incorruptible, and undefiled, and that fadeth not away" (1 Peter 1:4). If we seek, like the people of the world, to increase our possessions, those who are not believers may question whether we believe what we say about our inheritance and our heavenly calling.

Our Lord says that the earth is a place "where moth and rust doth corrupt, and where thieves break through and steal." All that is of the earth, and in any way connected with it, is subject to corruption, change, and dissolution. No reality or substance exists in anything but heavenly things. Often the careful amassing of earthly possessions ends in losing them in a moment by fire, robbery, or a change in the world markets. Furthermore, in a little while, we all must leave this earth, or the Lord Jesus will return. What use will earthly possessions be then?

Our Lord, however, does not merely tell us not to lay up treasure on earth. If He had said no more, people may abuse this commandment and use it to encourage extravagant habits, spending everything they have or can obtain *upon themselves*. Jesus does not mean that we should live up to our income. He adds, "But lay up for yourselves treasures in heaven." Every penny given for the Lord's sake to poor brethren or to the work of God is a treasure laid up in the bank of heaven. When we go to heaven, we go to the place where our treasures are, and we shall find them there.

The Lord concludes: "For where your treasure is, there will your heart be also." Where should the heart of the disciple of the Lord Jesus be, but in heaven? Our calling is a heavenly calling, our inheritance is a heavenly inheritance, and our citizenship is in heaven. But if we believers in the Lord Jesus lay up treasures on earth, then our hearts will be on earth. Laying up treasures in heaven will draw the heart heavenward. It brings along with it, even in this life, precious spiritual blessings as a reward of obedience to the commandment of our Lord.

November 13. I took one shilling out of the box in my house. This shilling was all our money for today. More than a hundred people must be provided for, and this is not the case once in a while, but very frequently. It is infinitely precious to have the living God as a Father to go to for help. Everyone who believes in the Lord Jesus may claim His help since we are all children of God. "For ye are all the children of God by faith in Christ Jesus" (Galatians 3:26). Although all believers in the Lord Jesus are not called upon to establish orphan houses and schools for poor children and to trust in God for means, all believers should cast all their care upon Him who cares for them. We need not be anxiously concerned about anything. (See 1 Peter 5:7, Philippians 4:6, and Matthew 6:25-34.)

Under these circumstances of need, a silver watch, which had become the property of the orphan fund yesterday afternoon, was sold to help us through the expenses of today.

The coal is almost gone in each of the houses, and every article of provision is greatly reduced. Truly, we are exceedingly poor. Nevertheless, we have the necessary provisions until Monday morning, and thus we are brought to the close of another week. This afternoon, all the workers met for prayer.

November 14. When we met again this afternoon for prayer, we had reason to praise, for the Lord had sent financial help.

November 15. Last Friday, brother Craik and I had a meeting for inquirers into the faith and new fellowship members. We spoke with eight of them and had to send away ten since our strength was gone. This evening we saw seven and had to send away three.

December 9. We are now at the close of the sixth year of this part of the work. We are left with only the money which has been put aside for the rent. But throughout the year, we have been supplied with all that was needed.

During the last three years, we had closed the accounts on this day and held public meetings stating how the Lord had dealt with us during the year. The substance of those meetings was later printed for the benefit of the Church at large. This time, however, it appeared better to delay both the public meetings and the publishing of the report. Through grace we had learned to lean on the Lord only. If we never spoke or wrote one single word about this work, we would be supplied with means as long as we depended on Him. What better proof could we give of our dependence on the living God alone and not on public meetings or printed reports than that, in the midst of our deep poverty, we still went on working quietly without saying anything. Naturally, we would have been glad to expose our poverty. But spiritually we were able to delight in the prospect of the increased blessing that might be derived by the Church as we continue to express our needs to God alone.

December 23. In reading over my journal this year, I found that the Lord has given me many precious answers to prayer. On May 23 I began to ask the Lord to deliver a certain sister from the great spiritual depression she was suffering. After three days, the Lord granted my request.

During this year one of the greatest sinners I had ever known in all my service for the Lord was converted. Repeatedly, I prayed with his wife for him. She came to me in deep distress on account of the cruel treatment she received from him because she wanted to live for the Lord. Her refusal to respond to his anger only infuriated him more.

At the time when the situation was at its worst, I pleaded the promise in Matthew 18:19: "Again I say unto you, that if two of you shall agree on earth as touching any thing that they shall ask, it shall be done for them of my Father which is in heaven." And now this awful persecutor has been converted!

On May 25 I began to ask the Lord for greater spiritual prosperity among the saints in Bristol than ever. Praise the Lord, He truly has answered this request. At no period has there been more manifestation of grace, truth, and spiritual power among us than there is now.

Chapter 15

DAILY PRAYER AND TIMELY ANSWERS

January 3, 1842. This evening we had a precious prayer meeting. When the usual time for closing the meeting came, some of us wanted to continue to wait upon the Lord. I suggested that those who had bodily strength, time, and a desire to wait longer upon the Lord, do so. At least thirty remained, and we continued in prayer until after ten. I never knew deeper prayer in the Spirit. I experienced an unusual nearness to the Lord and was able to pray in faith, without doubting.

January 4. The Lord has answered all our requests concerning the daily needs of the orphans. We have had an abundance these last several days, but the expenses have been great also.

February 5. We have only received as much as needed to provide for the orphans each day, and there is again great need. Now, at twelve o'clock, no means exist, as yet, to meet the expenses of today. The words in the prayer of Jehoshaphat in 2 Chronicles 20:12, "Neither know we what to do:

but our eyes are upon thee," are at this moment the language of my heart. I likewise do not know what to do, but my eyes are on the Lord. I am sure that He will help us this day also.

Evening. In the morning one pound ten shillings came in through the sale of some articles. We were able to supply all that was needed for today.

February 8. Enough food is in all the houses for the meals of today. But we have not been able to buy any bread, and there is not enough money to buy milk tomorrow morning. Coal is also needed in two houses. Indeed, as far as I know, we were never in greater poverty. But I am fully assured that the Lord will not leave us.

Evening. The Lord has not yet sent us what is needed for tomorrow, but He has given us fresh proof that He is mindful of us. This afternoon nine plum cakes were sent by a sister as a treat for the orphans. These cakes were an encouragement to me to continue to look out for further supplies. The little donations that came in today are precious, but they are not enough to meet the need of tomorrow. Before nine o'clock tomorrow morning we need more money to be able to buy milk. Truly, we are poorer than ever. Through grace my eyes do not look at the meager supplies and the empty purse, but to the riches of the Lord only.

February 9. I went to the Orphan Houses to see whether the Lord had sent in anything. When I arrived, I found that He had just sent help two or three minutes earlier. A brother was on his way to work this morning when the Lord put the orphans on his heart. The brother said to himself, "I cannot go there now. I will take something to them this evening." Nevertheless, he could not go on any further, but felt constrained to return and bring three sovereigns to the Orphan House. The Lord in His faithfulness helped us. Help was never more truly needed, nor did the help of the Lord ever come more obviously from Himself—His timing could not have been better.

Praise the Lord for His goodness! Praise Him that He helped us trust in Him in this trying hour.

February 12. Saturday. Today we were only able to supply the absolute necessities. When the mealtimes came, the Lord provided the food. Considering the great financial distress in our country, our dear orphans are very well provided for.

Of all the weeks during the last three years and seven months, this has been one of the most trying. Thanks to the Lord who has helped us this day also! Thanks to Him for enabling us to praise Him for the deliverance this morning. We were sure He would provide, and He did not disappoint us.

February 16. We had enough for breakfast, but nothing more came in during the morning. In the afternoon I again asked the Lord to send us help. I then sat down to meditate over the Word. I did not know whether there was a morsel of bread for tea in any of the houses, but I felt assured that the Lord would provide.

Through grace, my mind is fully assured of the

faithfulness of the Lord. In the midst of the greatest need, I am enabled to go about my other work in peace. Indeed, if the Lord did not give me this trust in Him, I would scarcely be able to work at all.

Soon after I sat down to meditate, a note was sent to me from the master of the orphan boys. He wrote, "When I visited the sisters in the Infant and Girls' Orphan Houses, I found them in the greatest need. There was no bread in one of the houses for tea this evening, and the six shillings sixpence was scarcely enough to supply what was needed for the dinner. I opened the offering box in the Boys' Orphan House and unexpectedly found one pound. Thus, through the kindness of the Lord, we were again abundantly supplied."

In the evening the Lord, in His love and faithfulness, blessed us again. I had preached at the meeting from the gospel of John. The last words on which I spoke were, "Said I not unto thee that if thou wouldest believe, thou shouldest see the glory of God?" (John 11:40). When the meeting was over, as a fresh proof of the truth of this Word, a note was given to me with five pounds for the orphans.

February 19. Saturday. Our money was again completely spent. Our provision stores were even more exhausted than on any previous Saturday. Not the least human likelihood remained for obtaining sufficient provisions for this *one* day, much less for *two* days.

When I went to the Orphan Houses before breakfast, I found a letter from Nottingham containing one shilling. This was not only a sweet proof that our Father remembered our need, but a promise that He would supply us with all we required this day. In the morning money came in, and we were provided with those things which were absolutely needed for this day.

February 25. This week was full of trials of faith, but also full of deliverances. Our need has never been greater than now. Most of the laborers felt considerably tried today, but the Lord has not allowed us to be discouraged. Through a remarkable circumstance, one of the laborers obtained some money this morning so that all the need of today could be amply met.

March 17. This morning our poverty, which now has lasted for several months, became exceedingly great. I left my house a few minutes after seven to go to the Orphan Houses to see whether there was enough money to buy milk. I prayed that the Lord would have mercy on us, even as a father has mercy on his children. I reminded Him of the consequences that would result, both in the lives of believers and unbelievers, if we had to give up the work because of lack of money, and that He therefore would not permit it to fail.

While I was walking and praying, I met a brother who was on his way to work. I greeted him and walked on, but he ran after me and gave me one pound for the orphans. Thus the Lord speedily answered my prayer.

Truly, it is worth being poor and greatly tried in faith for the sake of having such precious, daily proof of the loving interest which our kind Father takes in everything that concerns us. How could our Father do otherwise? He gave us the greatest possible proof of His love when He gave us His own Son. Surely He will also freely give us all things. (See Romans 8:32.)

If the hearts of the children of God are comforted and their faith strengthened, it is worth being poor and greatly tried in faith. Those who do not know God may read or hear of His dealings with us and see that faith in God is more than a mere notion. There is indeed reality in Christianity.

April 12. We were never in greater need than today, when I received one hundred pounds from the East Indies. It is impossible to describe the joy in God it gave me. My prayer this morning had been that our Father would now at last send larger sums of money. I was not in the least surprised or excited when this donation came, for I took it as the answer to prayer we had been expecting.

May 10. Our trials of faith during these seventeen months lasted longer and were sharper than during any previous period. Yet, the orphans had everything they needed in the way of nourishing food and clothing. We look back at the trials of our faith with perfect joy and peace, knowing that our God did not fail us even once. In our dependence on Him for every need, we have come to know in a fuller way that we are truly partners with Him in this work. "And truly our fellowship is with the Father, and with his Son Jesus Christ" (1 John 1:3).

The words *fellowship, communion,* and *partnership* mean the same. The believer in the Lord Jesus does not only obtain forgiveness of all his sins through the shed blood of Jesus, by faith in His name; he does not only become righteous before God, through the righteousness of the Lord Jesus; he is not only born of God, a partaker of the divine nature, and therefore a child of God and an heir of God; but he is also in fellowship or partnership with God. Just as God's love to His children is unalterably the same, so it is also with our fellowship or partnership with Him—it remains unalterably the same so far as God is concerned.

All that we possess in God as His partners may be brought down into our daily life and be enjoyed, experienced, and used. We may make unlimited use of our partnership with the Father and with the Son and draw out, by prayer and faith, the inexhaustible fullness in God.

If I were a businessman and found myself daily making the wrong decisions, what could I do? In myself there is no solution to the problem. I can expect nothing but further mistakes. And yet, I need not despair because the living God is my partner. I do not have sufficient wisdom to meet these difficulties, but He is able to direct me. I can pour out my heart to God and ask Him to guide and direct me and to supply me with wisdom. Then I have to believe that He will do so. I can go with good courage to my business and expect help from Him in the next difficulty that may come before me. As I do, I find that I am truly in partnership with the Father and with the Son.

If I desire more power over temptations, more wisdom, grace, or anything else that I may need in my service for God, what else should I do but make use of my fellowship with the Father and with the Son? By prayer and faith we may obtain all necessary temporal and spiritual help and blessings. In all simplicity, we can pour out our heart before God. Then we have to believe that He will give to us according to our need.

Do not let the consciousness of your unworthiness keep you from believing what God has said concerning you. If you are a believer in the Lord Jesus, then this precious privilege of being in partnership with the Father and the Son is yours.

Chapter 16

FOOD FOR GROWING FAITH

I desire that all the children of God who read this account of God's work in Bristol be led to trust Him for everything they need under any circumstances. I pray that the many answers to prayer we have seen may encourage them to pray, particularly for the conversion of their friends and relatives, their own growth in grace and knowledge, the saints whom they know personally, the state of the Church, and the success of the preaching of the gospel. Especially, I affectionately warn them against being led away by the deception of Satan to think that these things are peculiar to me and cannot be enjoyed by all the children of God.

All believers are called upon, in the simple confidence of faith, to cast all their burdens on God and to trust Him for everything. They should not only make everything a subject of prayer, but expect answers to their petitions which they have asked according to His will and in the name of the Lord Jesus. I do not have *the gift of faith* mentioned in 1 Corinthians 12:9 along with the gifts of healing, the working of miracles, and prophecy. It is true that the faith which I am able to exercise is God's own gift. He alone supports it, and He alone can increase it. Moment by moment, I depend on Him. If I were left to myself, my faith would utterly fail.

My faith is the same faith which is found in every believer. It has been increasing little by little for the last twenty-six years. Many times when I could have gone insane from worry, I was in peace because my soul believed the truth of that promise—"We know that all things work together for good to them that love God" (Romans 8:28).

When my brother and my dear father died, I had no evidence that they were saved. But I dare not say that they are lost, for I do not know. My soul was perfectly at peace under this trial, which is one of the greatest a believer can experience. I laid hold of that promise, "Shall not the Judge of all the earth do right?" (Genesis 18:25). This word, together with the whole character of God, as He has revealed Himself in His holy Word, settled all questionings. I believed what He has said concerning Himself and have been at peace ever since concerning this matter.

When sometimes all has appeared to be dark in my ministry, I could have been overwhelmed in grief and despair. At such times I was encouraged in God by faith on His almighty power, His unchangeable love, and His infinite wisdom. I said to myself, "God is able and willing to deliver me." It is written, "He that spared not his own Son, but delivered him up for us all, how shall he not with him also freely give us all things?" (Romans 8:32). This promise kept my soul in peace.

When trials have come against me which were far heavier than the financial needs; when lying reports were spread that the orphans did not have enough to eat or were cruelly treated; or when greater trials came in connection with this work, and I was nearly a thousand miles away from Bristol week after week; at such times my soul was stayed upon God. I believed His promises, and I poured out my soul before Him. I could rise from my knees in peace because the trouble was cast upon God.

By the grace of God, I do not boast in speaking this way. I give the glory to God alone that He has enabled me to trust in Him, and He has not permitted my confidence in Him to fail. No one should think that my depending on God is an unusual gift given to me, which other saints have no right to expect.

Trusting in God means more than obtaining money by prayer and faith. By the grace of God, I desire that my faith extend toward *everything*—the smallest of my own temporal and spiritual concerns, my family, the saints among whom I labor, the Church at large, and everything that has to do with the temporal and spiritual prosperity of the Scriptural Knowledge Institution.

I thank God for the faith He has given me, and I ask Him to uphold and increase it. Do not let Satan deceive you into thinking that *you* could not have the same faith. When I lose something like a key, I ask the Lord to direct me to it; and I look for an answer to my prayer. When a person with whom I have made an appointment is late, and I am inconvenienced, I ask the Lord to hasten him to me. When I do not understand a passage of the Word of God, I lift up my heart to the Lord that He would, by His Holy Spirit, instruct me. I expect to be taught, although I do not fix the time and the manner it should be. When I am going to minister the Word, I seek help from the Lord. While I am conscious of my natural inability as well as utter unworthiness, I am confident and cheerful because I look for His assistance and believe that He will help me.

You may do the same, dear believing reader! Do not think that I am extraordinary or that I have privileges above God's other dear children. I encourage you to try it! Stand firm in the hour of trial, and you will see the help of God, if you trust in Him. When we forsake the ways of the Lord in the hour of trial, the food for faith is lost.

This leads me to the following important point. You ask, "How may I have my faith strengthened?" The answer is this: "Every good gift and every perfect gift is from above, and cometh down from the Father of lights, with whom is no variableness, neither shadow of turning" (James 1:17). The increase of faith is a good gift, and it must come from God. Therefore, we should ask Him for this blessing.

The following guidelines will help a believer build his faith:

1. Carefully read the Word and meditate on it. Through reading the Word of God, and especially through meditation on it, the believer becomes acquainted with the nature and character of God. Besides God's holiness and justice, he realizes what a kind, loving, gracious, merciful, mighty, wise, and faithful Father He is. Therefore, in poverty, affliction, death of loved ones, difficulty in service, or financial need, he will rest on the ability of God to help him. He has learned from the Word that God is almighty in power, infinite in wisdom, and ready to help and deliver His people. Reading the Word of God, together with meditation on it, is an excellent way to strengthen faith.

2. We must maintain an upright heart and a good conscience and not knowingly and habitually indulge in things which are contrary to the mind of God. How can I possibly continue to act in faith if I grieve the Lord and detract from His glory and honor? All my confidence in God and all my leaning on Him in the hour of trial will be gone if I have a guilty conscience and yet continue in sin. If I cannot trust in God because of a guilty conscience, my faith is weakened.

With every fresh trial, faith either increases by trusting God and getting help, or it decreases by not trusting Him. A habit of self-dependence is either defeated or encouraged. If we trust in God, we do not trust in ourselves, our fellowmen, circumstances, or in anything else. If we *do* trust in one or more of these, we *do not* trust in God.

3. If we desire our faith to be strengthened, we should not shrink from opportunities where our faith may be tried. The more I am in a position to be tried in faith, the more I will have the opportunity of seeing God's help and deliverance. Every fresh instance in which He helps and delivers me will increase my faith. The believer should not shrink from situations, positions, or circumstances in which his faith may be tried, but he should cheerfully embrace them as opportunities to see the hand of God stretched out in help and deliverance. Thus his faith will be strengthened.

4. The last important point for the strengthening of our faith is that we let God work for us and do not work a deliverance of our own. When a trial of faith comes, we are naturally inclined to distrust God and to trust in ourselves, in our friends, or in circumstances. We would rather work a deliverance of our own than simply look to God and wait for His help. But if we do not patiently wait for God's help or if we work a deliverance of our own, then at the next trial of our faith we will have the same problem. We will again be inclined to try and deliver ourselves. With every fresh trial, our faith will decrease. On the contrary, if we stand firm in order to see the salvation of God,

trusting in Him alone, our faith will be increased. Every time we see the hand of God stretched out on our behalf in the hour of trial, our faith would be increased even more. God will prove His willingness to help and deliver at the perfect time.

Scriptural principles may be used to overcome the difficulties in business or any earthly calling. The children of God, who are strangers and pilgrims on earth, should expect to have difficulty in the world, for they are not at home here. But the Lord has provided us with promises in His Word to cause us to triumph over circumstances. All difficulties may be overcome by acting according to the Word of God.

Chapter 17

A TIME OF PROSPERITY

December 1, 1842. For the last several months, money and supplies have continued to flow in without interruption as they were needed. There was no excess or lack. But nothing came in today except five shillings for needlework. We only had enough to supply our absolute need—milk. We were unable to purchase the usual quantity of bread.

Someone may ask, "Why don't you buy the bread on credit? What does it matter whether you pay immediately for it or at the end of the month? Since the Orphan Houses are the work of the Lord, can't you trust Him to supply you with money to pay the bills from the butcher, baker, and grocer? After all, the things you purchase are needed so that the work may continue."

My reply is this: If this work is the work of God, then He is surely able and willing to provide for it. He will not necessarily provide at the time *we think* that there is need. But when there is real need, He will not fail us. We may and should trust in the Lord to supply us with what we require at present, so that there may be no reason to go into debt.

I could buy a considerable amount of goods on credit, but the next time we were in need, I would turn to further credit instead of turning to the Lord. Faith, which is maintained and strengthened only by *exercise,* would become weaker and weaker. At last, I would probably find myself deeply in debt with no prospect of getting out of it.

Faith rests on the written Word of God, but there is no promise that He will pay our debts. The Word says, "Owe no man any thing" (Romans 13:8). The promise is given to His children, "I will never leave thee, nor forsake thee" (Hebrews 13:5). "He that believeth on him shall not be confounded" (1 Peter 2:6). We have no scriptural grounds to go into debt.

Our goal is to show the world and the Church that even in these last evil days, God is ready to help, comfort, and answer the prayers of those who trust in Him. We need not go to our fellowmen or to the ways of the world. God is both able and willing to supply us with all we need in His service.

Through the printed accounts of this ministry, many have been converted. We consider it our precious privilege to continue to wait upon the Lord only instead of buying goods on credit or borrowing money from kind friends. As God gives us grace we will look to Him only, although from meal to meal we have to depend on Him. God is now in the tenth year of feeding these orphans, and He has never allowed them to go hungry. He will care for them in the future also.

I am deeply aware of my own helplessness and dependence on the Lord. Through the grace of God my soul is in peace, although day after day we have to wait on the Lord for our daily bread.

December 16. Nothing has come in. At six o'clock this evening, our need was very great in the Orphan Houses and the day schools. I prayed with two of the laborers. We needed some money to come in before eight o'clock tomorrow morning, so that we could buy milk for breakfast. Our hearts were at peace, and we felt assured that our Father would supply our need.

We had scarcely risen from our knees when I received a letter containing a sovereign for the orphans. About five minutes later, a brother promised to give me fifty pounds next week. A quarter of an hour after that, a brother gave me a sovereign, which a sister in the Lord had left for the orphans. How sweet and precious it is to see the willingness of the Lord to answer the prayers of His needy children!

February 11, 1843. We had one pound fourteen shillings available to meet the expenses of this day. But since this was not enough, I asked the Lord for help; and this morning's mail brought me two pounds from Stafford. We now have enough for this day.

God's timing is always perfect. Why did this money not come a few days sooner or later? Because the Lord wanted to help us by it, and He influenced the donor just then, not sooner or later, to send it. Surely, all who know the Lord must see His hand in this work. I do not mean to say that it would be acting against the precepts of the Lord to seek for help in His work by personal and individual requests to *believers*. But I operate the ministry this way for the benefit of the Church at large. I cheerfully bear the trials and the precious joys of this life of faith if at least some of my fellowbelievers might see that a child of God does have power with Him by prayer and faith. That the Lord should use for so glorious a service one as unfaithful and unworthy as I am, can only be ascribed to the riches of His grace. He uses the most unlikely instruments so that the honor may be His alone.

March 8. On October 25, 1842, I had a long conversation with a sister in the Lord who seemed to be in a time of great financial need. I told her that my house and my money were hers. I had every reason to believe that she did not even have five pounds of her own. She assured me that she possessed five hundred pounds, and that it never seemed right to give away this money. She believed that God put this sum into her hands without her seeking, and she thought it was a provision which the Lord had made for her. I made no reply to this. She asked me to pray for her about how she should use this money.

After she left, I asked the Lord to cause her to realize the true riches and inheritance in the Lord Jesus and the reality of her heavenly calling. I asked that she would cheerfully lay down this five hundred pounds at His feet. I prayed about the matter daily for twenty-two days without mentioning it to anyone else. It would be far better that she kept this money than give it up and later regret the step she had taken and thereby dishonor the name of the Lord.

One day she was waiting to see me when I came home. She said she had sought the Lord's will concerning the five hundred pounds. She examined the Scriptures, prayed about it, and was now assured that it was His will for her to give up this money. I exhorted her to count the cost and insisted she wait at least two weeks longer before she carried out her intention.

She agreed. Eighteen days later, I received a letter from her. She was ready to give the money to our work in Bristol, but there would be several month's delay before it would be available to me. Naturally, I could have been very disappointed because I already had many ways in mind to use the money. But the Lord continued to meet our needs while I waited confidently on Him.

Day after day passed, and the money did not come. At last, on the one hundred and thirty-fourth day since I had *daily* sought the Lord about

165

this matter, I received a letter from the sister. She informed me that five hundred pounds had been paid into the hands of my bankers. She wrote in her letter, "I am thankful to say that I have never for one moment had the slightest feeling of regret, but it is wholly of the Lord's abounding grace. I speak it to His praise."

Several weeks later when I visited the Orphan Houses, one of the sisters mentioned that a young woman who lived with her father on Wilson Street wanted to move to a smaller house. She thought I may be interested in renting their house for the orphans. The sister had replied that she was sure that I had no thought of opening another Orphan House.

The more I pondered the matter, the more it appeared to me that this was the hand of God moving me onward in this service. The following remarkable combination of circumstances struck me in particular:

1. More applications have been made for the admission of orphans, especially during the last few months, than we are able to meet. The houses are filled as much as the health of the children and of the laborers will permit.

2. If I did rent another house for orphans, it would be most desirable and convenient to be in the same street where the other three are. But since the third Orphan House was opened, none of the larger houses in the street have been available.

3. Fifteen of the children in the Infant Orphan

House should be moved to the house for the older girls, but there is no room. When a vacancy happens to occur in that house, several children are waiting to fill it. My original intention was to move the children older than seven years to the houses for older boys and girls. Another Orphan House would solve the problem.

4. I know two sisters who would be suitable laborers for this fourth Orphan House, and they have a desire to be part of the work.

5. Three hundred pounds remain of the five hundred pounds I recently received. This money may be used to furnish a new Orphan House. I have never had this much money on hand at any one time during the last five years—a remarkable thing, in connection with the four other circumstances.

6. A fourth Orphan House would increase our expenses several hundred pounds a year. We have experienced almost continuous trials of faith for five years. This new Orphan House would prove that I have not regretted this service, and that I am not tired of depending on the Lord from day to day. The faith of other children of God might be strengthened and encouraged.

But as conclusive as these points were, they did not convince me that I should go forward in this service if the Spirit's leading did not accompany them. I therefore prayed day after day, *without saying anything to any other person*. I prayed twenty-two days without even mentioning it to my dear wife. Finally, I came to the conclusion that God wanted me to establish another Orphan House. That same day I received fifty pounds. What a striking confirmation that the Lord will help although the needs increase!

At last I went to inquire whether the woman still wanted to move to another house. But here I found an apparent hindrance. Since I had not expressed any interest in the house, she and her father changed their plans and decided to remain. But they asked me to come back in a week, and they would give me an answer.

I was not upset in the least by this obstacle. "Lord, if *You* have no need of another Orphan House, *I* have none," was my prayer. I was willing to do God's will and to delight myself in Him. I knew I was not seeking my own honor but the Lord's. I was not serving myself but Him. Through my times of prayer and waiting on the Lord, I had come to the conclusion that it was His will that I should go forward in this service. For these reasons I felt sure that I would have the house. I faced the obstacle in complete peace—a plain proof that I was being led by the Holy Spirit. If I had sought to enlarge the work by my own efforts, I would have been upset and uncomfortable.

After a week I called again on the woman. That same day her father had gone out and found a suitable house for them. He was willing to let me have the one on Wilson Street. I was accepted as a tenant, and all the difficulties were removed. After the first of June, we began getting the house ready; and in July, the orphans were received.

When a believer is doing the work that God has called him to do, he may be confident of success in spite of obstacles. The first thing he has to ask himself is: *Am I in a calling in which I can abide with God?* If you cannot ask God's blessing upon your occupation, or if you would be ashamed to be found in it when the Lord Jesus returns, or if it hinders your spiritual progress, then you must give it up and be engaged in something else. But this is only necessary in a few cases. Most occupations are not of such a nature that a believer would need to give them up in order to maintain a good conscience before God, although certain alterations may need to be made in the manner of conducting the business. The Lord will direct us in this if we wait upon Him and expect to hear His voice.

The next point to be settled is this: *Why do I carry on this business, or why am I engaged in this trade or profession?* In most instances the answer would be, "I am engaged in my earthly calling so that I may support myself and my family." Here is the chief error that causes almost all the other errors by children of God concerning their calling. To be engaged in a business *merely* to obtain the necessities of life for ourselves and family is not scriptural. *We should work because it is the Lord's will concerning us.* "Let him labour, working with his hands the thing which is good, that he may have to give to him that needeth" (Ephesians 4:28).

The Lord generally meets our needs through our jobs. But that is not *the reason* why we should work. If providing the necessities of life depended on our ability to work, we could never have freedom from anxiety. We would always have to say to ourselves, "What will I do when I am too old to work, or if I am sick?" But if we are engaged in our earthly calling because *it is the will of the Lord for us,* He is sure to provide for us because we labor in obedience to Him.

Why do I carry on this business? Why am I engaged in this trade or profession? These questions should first be settled in the fear of God and according to His revealed will. We will then answer honestly, "I carry on my business as a servant of Jesus Christ. He has commanded me to work, and therefore, I work." Whether a believer chooses to become a missionary, a teacher, a carpenter, or a businessman, he will be blessed and find satisfaction in his career—as long as he works in joyful obedience to the Lord.

Chapter 18

GOD BUILDS A MIRACLE

For nearly ten years I never had any desire to *build* an Orphan House. On the contrary, I preferred spending the funds which came in for present needs, enlarging the work according to the means the Lord gave.

But at the end of October, 1845, I was led to consider this matter in a way I had never done before. I received a letter from a gentleman who lived on the street where the four Orphan Houses were. He courteously informed me that the residents in the nearby houses were inconvenienced by the Orphan Houses on Wilson Street. He asked me to do what seemed best to me about the matter.

I was very busy that week, and I had scarcely any time to consider it further. On Monday morning, however, I set apart some hours for prayerful consideration of the subject. I wrote down the reasons which appeared desirable that the Orphan Houses should be *moved* from Wilson Street, and the reasons *against moving*.

Reasons For Moving From Wilson Street

1. The neighbors feel inconvenienced by the noise of the children during playtime. This complaint is neither without foundation nor unjust, although one could not find fault with the dear children on account of it. It would probably give me a headache if I lived next door to the Orphan Houses. I therefore should do to others as I want them to do for me. This point had never before appeared to me in so serious a light.

2. The greatness of the number of the residents in the houses has prevented the drains from working properly, and it has often affected the water in one or two of the neighbor's houses. These words, "Let not then your good be evil spoken of" (Romans 14:16), and "Let your moderation [willingness to yield] be known unto all men" (Philippians 4:5), seemed to be two important portions of the Word of God to be acted upon in this matter.

3. We have no proper playgrounds on Wilson Street. Our playground is only large enough for the children of one house at a time, but children in four houses should have the benefit of it. We cannot arrange for all the children to use the playground because meals, school hours, weather, and other hindrances interfere.

4. No ground is available for a garden near the Orphan Houses. By moving from Wilson Street and obtaining premises surrounded by farmland, we would be able to benefit the children. They would have a better opportunity for practical labor, and it would give the boys an occupation more suitable for them than knitting.

5. The country air would be much better for the health of the orphans than the polluted air in the city.

6. In times of sickness we are too confined in the houses on Wilson Street. We do not have a single spare room in any of the houses. Although the Lord has mercifully helped us through such times in the past, yet it has not been without inconvenience. We sometimes have more children in one room than is desirable for good health. Even when there is no sickness, it would be desirable to have more room.

The more I have considered the matter, the more I am persuaded that no ordinary large house, built only to accommodate ten people at most, will be suitable for a charitable institution of any considerable size. There seemed to me, therefore, no other choice but to build.

Reasons For Remaining On Wilson Street

1. God has plainly given us this location. As we have grown in size, God has opened up other houses on this street to be available for our use.

Until now God has pointed out Wilson Street as being the spot where this work should be carried on. Could the time have come for moving?

2. Perhaps we should rent more houses on Wilson Street. We could use two houses for Orphan Houses and one of them for an infirmary in case of sickness. (But then the objection of the neighbors would remain on account of the noise of the children. The drains would be more unsuitable since they are not constructed for so many residents. To alter them would be a heavy expense. The playground would be even less sufficient. Lastly, there is no reason to think that we could rent any additional houses.)

3. Three great objections exist against building. A considerable sum is required which could be spent for the orphans' present needs. The pilgrim character of the Christian seems to be lost in building a permanent structure. Finally, it will take a great deal of time to make the necessary arrangements for it.

But all these objections only hold good if I *needlessly* set about building. If I could rent premises which are in every way suitable for the work, and I still *preferred* to build, then those objections would apply to this case. But we could not be accused of needlessly spending money in building instead of renting. Neither would time be wasted. Therefore, these three objections just mentioned were removed once I saw plainly that no other choice remained but to build.

After I had spent a few hours in prayer and consideration over the subject, I began to see that the Lord was leading me to build. His intentions were to benefit the orphans and better order of the whole work. Furthermore, He wanted to show that He could and would provide large sums for those who need them and trust in Him for them. During no period had the number of the applications for the admission of orphans been greater than just before I was led to think about building.

That same afternoon, I laid the matter before my fellow-laborers in the church to get their opinion. They were all in agreement that they saw no reason not to build. The next day, my dear wife and I began to meet for prayer about this matter and planned to do so every morning. We asked God for clearer light concerning the details of the project. Being assured that it was His will that I should build, I began asking the Lord for money.

Sufficiently large premises to accommodate three hundred children would be needed, together with a large piece of ground near Bristol for the building and a small farm. This would cost at least ten thousand pounds. I was not discouraged by this but trusted in God.

We continued meeting for prayer every morning for fifteen days, but not a single donation came in. But my heart was not discouraged. The more I prayed, the more assured I was that the Lord would provide. It is as if I had already seen the new premises actually before me. Since the beginning of the Scriptural Knowledge Institution, God has led me forward and enlarged the work without my seeking after it. My only motives are the honor and glory of God, the welfare of the Church, the physical and spiritual welfare of destitute orphans, and the welfare of all those who would take care of them. After praying again and again about the matter, I still remained in perfect peace. I therefore decided it was assuredly God's will that I should go forward.

On November 15 a brother arrived to work for a little while in Bristol. I told him about having to move the orphans from Wilson Street. He felt that it was God's will that I build. This dear brother's judgment greatly encouraged me. He also suggested that I seek God's direction for the design of the building. He said, "You must ask help from God to show you the plan, so that all you do may be according to the mind of God."

I waited daily upon God for finances for this work, and not a single penny had been given to me. Nevertheless, this did not discourage me. My assurance increased more and more that God, in His own time and in His own way, would give the means.

More than at any period in my life, I was struck by these verses: "My brethren, count it all joy when ye fall into divers temptations; Knowing this, that the trying of your faith worketh patience. But let patience have her perfect work, that ye may be perfect and entire, wanting nothing"

(James 1:2-4). These words spoke to my heart about building the Orphan House. I asked the Lord to increase my faith and sustain my patience. I knew that I needed patience as well as faith.

On the thirty-sixth day after I began to pray, I received one thousand pounds for building the Orphan House. It was the largest single donation I had ever received. But I was as calm and quiet as if I had only received one shilling because I was expecting to receive an answer to my prayers. Even if five thousand pounds or ten thousand pounds had been given to me, it would not have surprised me.

December 13. My sister-in-law told me that she met a gentleman in London who read the story of the Lord's dealings with me. She told him that I planned to build an Orphan House, and he, an architect, offered to make the plan and supervise the building gratuitously. He is also a Christian. The fact that this offer comes unsolicited and from a Christian architect especially shows the hand of God.

December 23. This is now the fiftieth day since I have come to the conclusion to build. Not even one penny has come in since December 10. This morning I have been particularly encouraged because the Lord sent me the one thousand pounds and the promise from that Christian architect whose name I don't even know yet.

I have begun to be more specific in my prayers. We should have a large piece of ground, at least six or seven acres, in the vicinity of Bristol. This will, of course, be very expensive, but my hope is in God. I have not sought after this thing, nor has it begun with me. God has unexpectedly led me to it. The day before I received my neighbor's letter making me aware of the inconveniences caused by the orphans, I had no thought about building a house for the orphans. My prayer is that God will continue to give me faith and patience. If He helps me to wait on Him, help will surely come.

December 24. No further donations have come in, but my hope in God is unshaken. He most assuredly will help. I have purposely not printed any information in connection with this matter, in order that the hand of God may be clearly seen. I spoke to a few people about my intention of building, when the conversation led to it. Through this, the Lord can make it known to others and thus send money for the building fund. Or He can send in such an abundance for the work which is already in existence that there might be a rich surplus for the building fund. No doubt, we will face many trials connected with this enlargement of the field of labor. Therefore, I desire to see clearly that God Himself is leading me onward.

December 29. This evening I received fifty pounds. This donation is exceedingly precious to me not only because it was cheerfully given, nor even because of its size, but because it is another precious proof that God will provide for the building. My assurance has been increasing that

God will build for Himself a large Orphan House in this city to show what a blessed thing it is to trust in Him. I can only say, "Lord, here is Your servant, if You want to use me."

December 30. This morning I came, in the course of my reading, to the book of Ezra. I was particularly refreshed by the two following points in the first chapter, and I applied them to the building of the Orphan House.

1. Cyrus, an *idolatrous* king, was used by God to provide the means for building the temple at Jerusalem. How easy it would be for God to provide ten thousand pounds for the Orphan House or even twenty or thirty thousand pounds if needed.

2. The people were stirred up by God to help those who went up to Jerusalem. It is a small matter for Him to put it into the hearts of His children to help me.

January 3, 1846. One of the orphans gave six-pence for the building fund. This morning I asked the Lord to go before me, and I went out to look for a piece of ground. The armory had been mentioned to me several times as a suitable place. I did not think so, yet I thought I should at least look at it. After I saw it, my judgment about its unsuitableness was confirmed. On my way back to the city, I saw some fields near the armory. This evening I have been led to write to the owner, asking whether he wants to sell them. I am now quietly waiting for the Lord's further direction. If His time has come to answer our requests for a suitable piece of land, I will be glad. If not, I desire that patience may have her perfect work.

January 8. I received a reply to my letter. The owner of the fields writes that the land is too expensive for me to afford.

January 9. I went to see those fields again, and they seem very suitable. I met a land agent there who told me that they would be nearly a thousand pounds per acre and, therefore, too expensive. I asked the agent to inform me if he heard of any suitable land for sale.

January 31. It is now eighty-nine days since I have been daily waiting upon God about the building of an Orphan House. The Lord will soon give us a piece of ground, and I told the brothers and sisters so this evening.

February 2. Today I heard of suitable and inexpensive land on Ashley Down.

February 3. The land on Ashley Down is the best of all I have seen.

February 4. This evening I called on the owner of the land on Ashley Down, but he was not at home. I was told that I could find him at his business. I went there, but he had left a few minutes earlier. I could have gone back to his house, but I did not do so, judging that it was God's will that I did not find him at either place. I decided not to force the matter but to "let patience have her perfect work."

February 5. This morning I saw the owner of the land. He told me that he awoke at three o'clock this morning and could not sleep again until five. While he was lying awake, he kept thinking about the piece of land he had heard I wanted for the Orphan House. He decided that if I want to buy it, he would let me have it for one hundred and twenty pounds per acre, instead of two hundred pounds, the price which he had previously asked. How good the Lord is! The agreement was made this morning, and I purchased a field of nearly seven acres.

February 8. I wrote to the architect who has offered his help.

February 11. I received a reply to my letter to the architect. He was happy to offer his abilities as an architect and surveyor, free of charge, to help us build the new Orphan House.

The total amount given for the building fund, as of June 4, 1846, is a little over two thousand seven hundred pounds. This is only a small part of what will be needed; but God, in His own time, will send the whole sum. Two hundred and twelve days have passed since I first began to pray about this work. I am more than ever assured that God will condescend to use me to build this house. If I had made this decision based on mere enthusiasm, I would have been overwhelmed by the difficulties. But God has led me to this work. He has helped me in the past and will continue to help me until the end.

July 4. My faith and patience have been exceedingly tried. Great difficulties arose about my possessing the land after all. But, by God's grace, my heart was kept in peace, being fully assured that if the Lord took this piece of land from me, it would only be for the purpose of giving me a still better one. Our heavenly Father never takes anything from His children unless He means to give them something better.

In the midst of this great trial of faith, I could not help thinking that the difficulties were only allowed for the trial of my faith and patience. Last evening I received a letter stating that all the difficulties were removed. In a few days, the deed will be transferred.

July 6. The reason why so little came in for the building fund during the last several months seems to be that we did not need the money at that time. When it was needed, and when my faith and patience had been sufficiently tried, the Lord sent more. Today two thousand and fifty pounds were given to me—two thousand pounds for the building fund and fifty pounds for present expenses.

It is impossible to describe my joy in God when I received this donation. I expect answers to my prayers, and I believe that God hears me. Yet my heart was so full of joy that I could only sit before God and praise Him. At last I fell on my knees and burst forth in thanksgiving to God. I surrendered my heart afresh to Him for His blessed service.

November 19. This morning between five and six o'clock I prayed, among other things, about the building fund. I then had a long time for reading the Word of God. I came to Mark 11:24: "What things soever ye desire, when ye pray, believe that ye receive them, and ye shall have them." I have often spoken about the importance of the truth contained in this verse. Applying it to the new Orphan House, I said to the Lord, "Lord, I believe that You will give me all I need for this work. I am sure that I will have all, because I believe that I receive in answer to my prayer."

This evening a registered letter came for me containing a check for three hundred pounds. Two hundred and eighty pounds are for the building fund, ten pounds for my own personal expenses, and ten pounds for brother Craik. The Lord's holy name be praised for this precious encouragement! The building fund is now increased to more than six thousand pounds.

December 9. It is now four hundred days since I have been waiting upon God for help to build the Orphan House. But as yet He keeps me in the trial of faith and patience. He seems to be saying, "My hour is not yet come." Yet He does sustain me in continuing to wait upon Him. By His grace my faith is not in the least shaken. I am quite sure that He, in His own time, will give me everything I need concerning this work. How and when I will be supplied, I do not know. But I am sure that God will help me in His own time and way.

In the meantime I have abundant reason to praise God that I am not waiting on Him in vain. During this past year He has given me, in answer to prayer, a suitable piece of ground, and six thousand three hundred and four pounds for the building fund. Surely, I am not waiting upon the Lord in vain! By His help, then, I am resolved to continue this course to the end.

Chapter 19

ANSWERING GOD'S CALL TO SERVICE

January 25, 1847. The season is approaching when the building may begin. I have prayed with increased earnestness that the Lord would speedily send the remainder of the required amount. I believe the time is drawing near when the Lord will give me all I need to begin to build. I rose from my knees this morning in full confidence not only that God *could* but also *would* send the money soon.

About an hour after I had prayed, the sum of two thousand pounds was given to me for the building fund. I cannot describe the joy I had in God when I received this donation. I have waited four hundred and forty-seven days upon God for the amount we needed. How great is the blessing the soul obtains by trusting in God and by waiting patiently. From December 10, 1845 to January 25, 1847, I have received, solely in answer to prayer, nine thousand two hundred and eighty-five pounds. The Lord is willing to give what will be needed once the new Orphan House is built, although the expenses will be about two thousand five hundred pounds a year more than they were before.

From the opening of this institution it had been my desire to use part of the funds to aid missionaries who are not supported by regular salary. During the last two years, the Lord has allowed me to do so in a far greater degree than before. I know that many who preach the Word do not have any salary to live on and are in need.

Some may say that these people should trust in God. If they preach Jesus as the only hope for the salvation of sinners, they should set a good example by trusting God for the supply of their temporal necessities. This would encourage unconverted people to trust in the Lord Jesus for the salvation of their souls. But I also felt that I, as their brother, should try to help them as much as I could. My own money would go only a little way, so I began to pray more earnestly than ever for missionaries. The Lord answered my daily supplications, and I was honored to send nearly three times my usual amount of support to them.

I have asked God to direct me especially to send support to those who might be in particular need. I also tried to share with them an encouraging word to strengthen their hearts in God. These dear brethren have been helped not only by the money in a temporal way but also in the help that has refreshed and strengthened their hearts to trust in God even more.

March 9. How good is the Lord in helping me week after week through the heavy expenses, especially in this time of deep economic distress and scarcity of provisions! To His praise I can say we have lacked nothing all winter.

When *sight* ceases, it is the time for *faith* to work. The greater the difficulties, the easier it is for faith. As long as human possibilities for success remain, faith does not accomplish things as easily as when all natural prospects fail. During the time of poverty, our expenses were considerably greater than usual. Many people who otherwise might have supported us were unable to do so or had their surplus directed into other channels. But the gold and silver are the Lord's. To Him we made our prayer, and in Him we put our trust. He did not forsake us. We went as easily through that winter as through any other. God used this time as a special opportunity of showing the blessedness of trusting in Him.

May 11. I have been able to meet all the expenses connected with housekeeping during the coming week. The children have lacked nothing. Never were provisions as expensive as they are now. The bread and rice cost almost twice as much as eighteen months ago, and the oatmeal is nearly three times as expensive. No potatoes can be purchased because of the high prices.

In these days of financial struggles, the question

naturally arises, "If you only have to care for one hundred and thirty orphans, and you are so poor, what will you do when there are three hundred?" Such thoughts do not trouble me. The Lord can supply all the financial means that the work will require when the new Orphan House is opened, as easily as He does now.

July 7. Work on the building was begun today. Finally, after I sought the help of God for six hundred and seven days, He has given me the desire of my heart.

February 3, 1848. Someone may say, "You are continually in need. No sooner is the one demand met than another comes. Doesn't it seem like a trying life? Aren't you tired of it?"

I am more or less continually in need in connection with this work. God has supplied me with money to continue, and I enjoy telling people how He has answered my requests. But money is by no means the chief thing that I stand in need of from day to day.

Sickness among the children is always a difficult trial. Prayer is required for money, medicine, and guidance and wisdom from God.

Sometimes children are hired out as household help or apprentices. Finding a suitable place for them is important; however, it is more difficult than obtaining money. Sometimes I have waited upon God for many weeks to have this need supplied, but He has always helped.

Sometimes my need of wisdom and guidance is

great in order to know how certain children should be treated under particular circumstances. A need in this respect is no small thing, although I have been helped when I waited patiently on God.

When one of the laborers must leave the work on account of health or other reasons, I am in far greater need than when I require money for the institution. Such a need can only be supplied by waiting on God.

One of the greatest difficulties connected with this work is to find suitable godly persons for it. Many things are to be considered—suitable age, health, ability, experience, love for children, true godliness, preparation to bear with the many trials and difficulties connected with it, and a strong desire to labor, not for the sake of the money but to serve God.

To find godly persons with these qualifications is not an easy matter. I am not looking for perfect fellow-laborers, nor do I suppose that my fellow-laborers are without weaknesses, deficiencies, and failings. I myself am far from perfect. But I try to find suitable individuals in whom, as much as possible, the above qualifications are united.

The laborers should work happily among themselves, and then I can work easily with them. I must be their servant; and yet, I must maintain the place of authority God has given me over this work. This need is far greater than any that is connected with money. These matters lead a person to call upon God! Truly, I am in continual need.

Many years have passed since I made my boast in God by publishing reports of this ministry. Satan unquestionably is waiting for me to fall. If I was left to myself, I would fall prey to him at once. Pride, unbelief, or other sins would be my ruin and lead me to bring disgrace upon the name of Jesus. No one should admire me, be astonished at my faith, or think of me as if I were an amazing person. No, I am as weak as ever. I need to be upheld in faith and every other grace.

Nevertheless, I do not find that this work leads to a trying life but a very happy one. It is impossible to describe the abundance of peace and heavenly joy that often flows into my soul because of the answers I obtain from God after waiting on Him for help and blessing. The longer I have had to wait on Him, or the greater my need is, the greater the enjoyment when at last the answer came. I am not in the least tired of this way of life because I expected difficulties from the very beginning. For the glory of God and the encouragement of His dear children, I desired to pass through them, if only the saints might be benefited by the dealings of God with me.

The longer I go on in this service, the greater the trials of one kind or another become. But at the same time, I grow happier in my service and more assured that I am employed as the Lord would have me to be. How then could I be tired of carrying on the work of God? God has proved many times that He is faithful to His Word: "Seek ye first the kingdom of God, and his righteousness; and all these things shall be added unto you" (Matthew 6:33).

The great business which the disciple of the Lord Jesus has to be concerned about is to seek the Kingdom of God. I believe this means to seek the external and internal prosperity of the Church. If we seek to win souls for the Lord Jesus, we are seeking the *external* prosperity of the Kingdom of God. If we help our fellow-members in the Body grow in grace and truth or care for them in any way, we are seeking the *internal* prosperity of God.

In connection with this, we also have to seek His righteousness. This means to seek to be more and more like God—to seek to be inwardly conformed to the mind of God. If these two things are attended to diligently, we come to that precious promise: "And all these things [that is, food, clothing, or anything else you need for this present life] shall be added unto you."

Do you make it your primary business and your first great concern to seek the Kingdom of God and His righteousness? Are the things of God, the honor of His name, the welfare of His Church, the conversion of sinners, and the profit of your own soul, your chief aim? Or does your business, your family, or your own temporal concerns primarily occupy your attention? Remember that the world will pass away, but the things of God will endure forever. I never knew a child of God who acted according to the above passage for whom the Lord did not fulfill His promise, "All these things shall be added unto you."

April 29. The total amount that I have received for the building fund is more than eleven thousand pounds. This sum enables me to meet all the expenses connected with the purchase of the land and the building of the house. Praise the Lord!

Chapter 20

THE EXCITING LIFE OF STEWARDSHIP

May 1, 1848. Whether we are called as missionaries or another trade or profession, we should carry on our business as stewards of the Lord. The child of God has been bought with the precious blood of the Lord Jesus. All that he possesses—his bodily strength, his mental strength, his ability of every kind, his trade or business, and his property—all belong to God. It is written, "Ye are not your own. For ye are bought with a price" (1 Corinthians 6:19-20).

The proceeds of our calling are not our own in the sense of having freedom to spend them on the gratification of our pride or our love of pleasure. We have to stand before our Lord and Master as His stewards to seek His will concerning how He will have us use the proceeds of our calling. In 1 Corinthians 16:2, it is written, "Upon the first day of the week let every one of you lay by him in store, as God has prospered him." A contribution for the poor saints in Judea was to be made, and the brethren at Corinth were exhorted to give every Lord's day according to the measure of success which the Lord had blessed them during the week. Now, shouldn't the saints today also act according to this word? It is altogether in accordance with our pilgrim character to see how much we can afford to give to the poor or to the work of God every week.

We should also keep in mind the scriptural principle, "He which soweth sparingly shall reap also sparingly; and he that soweth bountifully shall reap also bountifully" (2 Corinthians 9:6). We are abundantly blessed in Jesus, and we need no stimulus to do good works. The forgiveness of our sins, having been made forever the children of God, having before us the Father's house as our home— these blessings should constrain us to serve God in love and gratitude all the days of our lives.

The verse is true, both in this life and in the life to come. If we have been sparingly using our property for Him, little treasure will be laid up in heaven. But if the love of Christ constrains a brother to sow bountifully, he will, even in this life, reap bountifully, both in blessings for his soul and in temporal things. "There is that scattereth, and yet increaseth; and there is that withholdeth more than is meet, but it tendeth to poverty. The liberal soul shall be made fat: and he that watereth shall be watered also himself" (Proverbs 11:24-25).

"Give, and it shall be given unto you; good measure, pressed down, and shaken together, and running over, shall men give into your bosom. For with the same measure that ye mete withal it shall be measured to you again" (Luke 6:38). This evidently refers to this life and temporal things.

Let us walk as *stewards* and not act as owners, keeping for ourselves the means with which the Lord has entrusted us. He has not blessed us that we may gratify our own carnal mind but for the sake of using our money in His service and to His praise.

A brother with small earnings may ask, "Should I also give? My earnings are already so small that my family can barely make ends meet."

My reply is, "Have you ever considered that the very reason your earnings remain so small may be because you spend everything on yourself? If God gave you more, you would only use it to increase your own comfort instead of looking to see who is sick or who has no work at all that you might help them."

A brother whose earnings are small may be greatly tempted to refuse the responsibility of assisting the needy and sick saints or helping the work of God. He thinks it should be the work of a few rich believers in the fellowship. Thus he robs his own soul!

How much should you give of your income? God lays down no rule concerning this point. We should give cheerfully and not because it is required. But if even Jacob, with the first dawning of spiritual light promised to God the tenth of all, how much should we believers in the Lord Jesus do for Him? (See Genesis 28:22). If the love of Christ causes us to give, we will have this verse fulfilled in our experience. The Lord will abundantly repay us, and in the end we will find that we are not losers even in temporal things. But the moment someone begins to give for the sake of receiving more back from the Lord, or he stops sowing bountifully in order to increase his own possessions, the river of God's bounty will no longer continue to flow.

The child of God must be willing to be a channel through which God's abundant blessings flow. This channel is narrow and shallow at first, yet some of the waters of God's bounty can pass through. If we cheerfully yield ourselves to this purpose, the channel becomes wider and deeper, allowing more of the bounty of God to pass through. We cannot limit the extent to which God may use us as instruments in communicating blessing if we are willing to yield ourselves to Him and are careful to give Him all the glory.

May 3. The work is now large, and the expenses are great. During the month we spent about five hundred pounds for the various supplies for the institution. I cannot expect the expenses to decrease—but I have no desire that they should! I have as much joy in writing checks for large amounts as I have in depositing the money which I receive from God through donors. The money is of no value to me unless I can use it for God. The more I pay out for the work of God, the more prospect I have of being further supplied by Him. The larger the sum I obtain from Him, in answer to prayer, the greater is the proof of the blessedness and the reality of dealing directly with God alone for what I need. Therefore, I have as much joy in giving as in receiving.

With all my might I have devoted myself to have the Orphan House filled with children. As large sums are needed and expended, I will have a greater reason than ever to draw upon the inexhaustible treasures of God. Obviously, money obtained by prayer may not be wasted. If anyone would obtain means from God by prayer and then waste it, he would soon find that he was not able to pray in faith for further supplies.

January 17, 1849. Further steps are to be taken to furnish the new Orphan House. More than two-thirds of the rooms are almost ready. I have prayed earnestly every day that the Lord would give me the money we still need. This evening I received six hundred pounds which will take care of the heavy expenses connected with furnishing the new Orphan House.

February 12. The new Orphan House is now almost entirely finished. In six weeks, with the help of God, all will be completed. I have been very busy during the last two weeks making the necessary arrangements for furnishing it. I began to pray still more earnestly that the Lord would give me the means which may yet be needed for the completion of the house.

A brother in the Lord came to me this morning and, after a few minutes of conversation, gave me two thousand pounds for furnishing the new Orphan House or for anything else needed in connection with the orphans. I have placed all of this sum, at least for the present, in the building fund.

Now I am able to meet all the expenses. In all probability I will even have several hundred pounds more than I need. The Lord not only gives as much as is absolutely necessary for His work, but He gives *abundantly*. This blessing filled me with inexpressible delight. He had given me the full answer to my thousands of prayers during these eleven hundred and ninety-five days.

February 26. After all the expenses had been met for the purchase of the land, the building, and furnishing of the new Orphan House, a balance remained of seven hundred and seventy-six pounds. This proved that the Lord can not only supply us with all we need in His service simply in answer to prayer, but He can also give us even more than we need.

June 18. Today, as the fruit of the prayers of three years and seven months, the children began to be moved from the four Orphan Houses in Wilson Street to the new Orphan House.

June 23. This has been a week of great blessing. All the orphans with their teachers and overseers have been moved into the new Orphan House.

About one hundred and forty people now live under one roof. The Lord has greatly helped us.

For more than three years, I have sought the help of God concerning everything connected with the new Orphan House. I expected His help, but He has done beyond my expectations. Although the last children were moved in only the day before yesterday, great order has already been established in the house, and everything is running smoothly. Praise the Lord for this! My soul magnifies Him for His goodness! Also, the Lord has met all the extraordinary expenses connected with moving the orphans from Wilson Street into the new Orphan House. I have more than five hundred pounds available to begin housekeeping in the new Orphan House. How true that those who trust in the Lord will not be disappointed! After many great trials of faith during the thirteen years and two months the orphans were at Wilson Street, the Lord brought us from out from there in comparative abundance. May His holy name be praised!

August 30. I received a fifty-pound note with these words: "I send you a fifty-pound note, half for the missions, and half for the orphans, unless you are in any personal need. If so, take five pounds for yourself. This will be the last large sum I will be able to send you. Almost all the rest is already *out at interest.*"

I took half of this fifty pounds for the orphans and half for missionaries. When the writer said, "the rest is already *out at interest,*" he meant that he had given it away for the Lord. Indeed that is the best way of using the money the Lord entrusts to us.

[Since that time I have received other large donations from the same man. He used his money for God, and God soon trusted him with another large sum, which he again used for the Lord. This did not surprise me at all. In whatever way God makes us His stewards, whether in temporal or spiritual things, if we act as *stewards* and not as *owners,* He will make us stewards over *more.*]

Chapter 21

A NEW VICTORY OF FAITH

December 5, 1850. It is now sixteen years and nine months since I began the Scriptural Knowledge Institution for Home and Abroad. This institution was very small in the beginning. Now it is so large that the current expenses are over six thousand pounds a year. The new Orphan House is inhabited by three hundred orphans, and a total of three hundred and thirty-five persons are connected with it. My work is abundant.

Despite this, I am thinking about laboring more than ever in serving poor orphans. This matter has been on my mind for the last ten days, and I have begun to pray about it. I am considering the construction of another Orphan House, large enough for seven hundred orphans, so that I might be able to care for a total of one thousand orphans. I have received two hundred and seven orphans within the last sixteen months and now have seventy-eight waiting for admission.

Most other charitable institutions for orphans

make the admission of a destitute orphan very difficult, if not impossible, if they do not have an influential person to sponsor them. In our case, nothing is needed but application to me. The poorest person, without influence, without friends, without any expense, no matter where he lives or which denomination he is affiliated with, may be admitted. Since it is difficult for poor people to get their orphan relatives admitted into ordinary establishments, I feel called to be the friend of the orphan.

The experience I have had in this service for fifteen years calls me to make use of my knowledge to the utmost of my power. No member of a committee or president of a society could possibly have the same experience unless he personally had been engaged in such a work for a number of years, as I have been.

If seven hundred more young souls could be brought under regular godly training, what blessed service that would be for the Kingdom of Christ! I began this work to show the world and the Church that God in heaven hears and answers prayer. This is better accomplished the larger the work is, provided I obtain the means simply through prayer and faith.

But thoughts of another character have occurred to me. I already have an abundance of work. My dear wife is also very busy. Nearly all of her time is occupied, directly or indirectly, with the orphans. Am I taking on too much for my bodily strength and my mental powers by thinking about another Orphan House? Am I going beyond the measure of my faith in thinking about enlarging the work? Is this a delusion of Satan, an attempt to cast me down from my place of usefulness by making me go beyond my capabilities? Is it a snare to puff me up in pride by attempting to build a large Orphan House?

I can only pray that the Lord would not allow Satan to gain an advantage over me. By the grace of God, my heart says, "Lord, if I could be sure that it is Your will that I go forward in this matter, I would do so cheerfully. On the other hand, if I could be sure that these are vain, foolish, proud thoughts and are not from You, I would forget the whole idea."

My hope is in God. He will help me and teach me. Based on His former dealings with me, however, it would not be surprising if He called me to enlarge work in this way. Lord, please teach me Your will in this matter.

December 11. This matter has constantly been on my heart. My soul would rejoice to go forward in this service if I was sure that the Lord would have me to do so. On the other hand, if I felt assured that the Lord wanted me to be satisfied with my present service and not pray about enlarging the work, I would be happy to do so. I only want to please Him.

As to outward circumstances, I have had nothing to encourage me. The income of the Scriptural

Knowledge Institution has been unusually small while the expenses have been great. This would mean nothing to me if I was sure that the Lord wanted me to go forward. The burden of my prayer, therefore, is that God would teach me His will. I desire to patiently wait for the Lord's time when He will shine His light on my path.

December 26. I had another special time for prayer to seek the will of God. But while I continue to ask the Lord to not allow me to be misled, I have no doubt that I should go forward. This is one of the biggest steps I have ever taken, and I cannot go about it with too much caution, prayerfulness, and deliberation. I am in no hurry. I could wait for years before taking one step toward this thing or speaking to anyone about it. On the other hand, I would set to work tomorrow if the Lord wanted me to. I seek the honor and glorious privilege to be used more by the Lord. I served Satan in my younger years, and I desire now to serve God with all my might during the remaining days of my earthly pilgrimage.

Vast multitudes of orphans need the basic necessities of life. I desire to be used by the Lord as an instrument in providing all the necessary temporal supplies not only for the three hundred now under my care but for seven hundred more. I want to provide scriptural instruction for a thousand orphans. When God provides me with a house for seven hundred orphans and with everything needed to support them, it will be obvious to all that God still hears and answers prayer. I will continue, day by day, to wait on Him in prayer concerning this thing until He commands me to act.

January 2, 1851. Last week I began reading from the book of Proverbs. My heart has been refreshed by the following passage: "Trust in the Lord with all thine heart; and lean not unto thine own understanding. In all thy ways acknowledge him, and he shall direct thy paths" (Proverbs 3:5-6). By the grace of God, I do acknowledge the Lord in my ways. I have the comfortable assurance that He will direct my paths concerning this new Orphan House.

"The integrity of the upright shall guide them: but the perverseness of transgressors shall destroy them" (Proverbs 11:3). My honest purpose is to give glory to God, and therefore, I expect to be guided by Him.

"Commit thy works unto the Lord, and thy thoughts shall be established" (Proverbs 16:3). I do commit my works to the Lord, and therefore, I expect that my thoughts will be established. My heart is calm, quiet, and assured that the Lord will use me further in the orphan work.

January 14. I have set apart this evening for prayer, asking the Lord once more not to allow me to be mistaken in this thing. I have considered all the reasons against building another Orphan House. For the sake of clarity, I wrote them down.

Reasons *against* establishing another Orphan House for seven hundred Orphans:

1. Would I be going beyond my spiritual capabilities? "For I say, through the grace given unto me, to every man that is among you, not to think of himself more highly than he ought to think; but to think soberly, according as God hath dealt to every man the measure of faith" (Romans 12:3).

If the Lord left me to myself, one tenth of the difficulties and trials I face would be enough to overwhelm me. But as long as He sustains me, I am carried through one difficulty after another. By God's help I would be able to bear other difficulties and trials. I expect an increase of faith with every fresh difficulty the Lord helps me through.

2. Would I be going beyond my physical and mental strength? Of all the objections against establishing another Orphan House, this is the only real difficulty. The whole management, direction, and vast correspondence of the Scriptural Knowledge Institution has depended on me alone these sixteen years and ten months. By hiring an efficient secretary, clerk, and an inspector of the schools, I might with God's help accomplish even more as the director.

3. If I felt sure that the present state of the Scriptural Knowledge Institution were to be the limit to my work, I would lay aside this thing at once. But I am not sure that I have reached God's limit. The Lord has helped me through all the difficulties in the past. Seeing this vast field of

usefulness before me, and since I have many applications for the admission of orphans, I long to be used still further.

4. Is it like "tempting God" to think of building another Orphan House for seven hundred more orphans? "Tempting God" means, according to the Bible, to limit Him in any of His attributes. I do not wish to limit His power or His willingness to give me all the means I need to build another large Orphan House.

5. How will I get the money for building this large Orphan House? Even if I did, how will I, at the same time, get the money for carrying on the work that already exists? Looking at the matter *naturally,* this is indeed a weighty objection. But while I have no hope of succeeding on my own, I am not in the least discouraged *spiritually.* God has the power to give me the thirty-five thousand pounds I will need and much more. Moreover, I delight in the greatness of the difficulty. I want to be fully assured from the very outset that I go forward in this matter according to the Lord's will. If so, He will give me the means; if not, I will not have them. I do not intend to ask anyone personally for help, but I will give myself to prayer as I have in the past.

6. Suppose I succeed in getting this large Orphan House built. How will I be able to provide for seven hundred more orphans? I am too much a businessman not to realize the seriousness of this question. If I only looked at the thing naturally, I

would admit that I am going too far. But spiritually, I see no difficulty at all. If I am able to build this second Orphan House, God will surely provide as He enables me to trust in Him for supplies.

7. Suppose I was able to obtain this large sum for building a house for seven hundred other orphans. Suppose I was able to provide for them during my lifetime. What would become of this institution after my death? My business is to serve my own generation with all my might. In this way I will best serve the next generation if the Lord Jesus tarries. He may come again soon. But if He tarries and I pass on before His return, my work will benefit the generation to come.

If this objection was a sound one, I should never have begun the orphan work at all for fear of what might become of it after my death. Thus all the hundreds of destitute children whom the Lord has allowed me to care for during the last fifteen years would not have been helped by me.

8. Would building another Orphan House cause me to be lifted up in pride? There is danger of this, even if I was not called to increase this ministry. One tenth of the honor the Lord has bestowed on me, and one tenth of service with which He has entrusted me, would be enough to puff me up with pride.

I cannot say that the Lord has kept me humble. But I can say that He has given me a hearty desire to give to Him all the glory and to consider it a great mercy on His part that He has used me in His service. I do not see, therefore, that fear of pride should keep me from going forward in this work. Rather, I ask the Lord to give me a humble attitude and never permit me to rob Him of the glory which is due to Him alone.

Reasons *for* establishing another Orphan House:

1. Many applications for admission continue to come in. I consider it a call from God for me to do everything in my power to provide a home and scriptural education for a greater number of orphans. I cannot refuse to help as long as I see a door opened by God.

2. The moral state of the poorhouses greatly influences me to go forward. I have heard from good authority that the children placed in these houses are corrupted by the immoral people who live there.

3. I am further encouraged by the great help which the Lord has given me in this blessed service. When I look at the small beginning and consider how the Lord has helped me for more than fifteen years in the orphan work, I am confident about going forward.

4. My experience and capabilities have grown with the work. As director of the work, under God, from its smallest beginnings, I am responsible to Him to use the abilities He has given me. These things, in connection with the former reasons,

seem to be a call from God to go forward in a greater degree than ever.

5. The spiritual benefit of more orphans is another reason why I feel called to go forward. I desire more for them than mere decency and morality. I want them to become useful members of society. We teach them to work and instruct them in useful skills for this life.

I cannot be satisfied with anything less than the orphans' souls being won for the Lord. Since this is the primary aim concerning the dear orphans, I long to be more extensively used than ever, even that I may have a thousand of them under my care.

7. My greatest desire is to show forth the glory of God and His readiness to hear prayer.

8. I am peaceful and happy in the prospect of enlarging the work. This perfect peace that I feel after all the heart-searching daily prayer and studying the Word of God would not be the case if the Lord had not intended to use me more.

Therefore, on the ground of the objections answered and these eight reasons for enlarging the work, I have come to the conclusion that it is the will of God that I should serve Him by enlarging this work.

January 4. The Lord has given me precious proof that He is delighted when we expect great things from Him. I have received three thousand pounds this evening—the largest donation I have ever had. Far larger sums are expected in order that it may be even more apparent that the best way to obtain financial means for the work of the Lord is simply to trust Him. My joy in God on account of this donation cannot be described. I take the money out of the hands of the living God. My soul is calm and peaceful, without any emotional excitement, although the donation is so large. Like a voice from heaven, it encourages me to build another Orphan House.

May 24. Ninety-two more orphans have applied for admission, and seventy-eight are already on the waiting list. This number increases rapidly as the work becomes more widely known. I will go forward in this service and build, to the praise and honor of the living God, another Orphan House large enough to accommodate seven hundred orphans. The greatness of the sum required to accomplish this work gives me special joy. The greater the difficulty to be overcome, the more it will be seen how much can be accomplished by prayer and faith. When God overcomes our difficulties for us, we have the assurance that we are engaged in His work and not our own.

Chapter 22

RECEIVING MORE TO GIVE MORE

May 26, 1851. The Christian should never worry about tomorrow or give sparingly because of a possible future need. Only the present moment is ours to serve the Lord, and tomorrow may never come. Money is really worth no more than as it can be used to accomplish the Lord's work. Life is worth as much as it is spent for the Lord's service.

Any occupation can be used to serve the Lord, but certain principles must be followed in secular work. The Christian must guard against any attitudes or practices that will keep him from experiencing God's abundant prosperity. God is not likely to bless anything that leads a believer to depend more on himself or his circumstances than on the living God. For example, the Christian businessman should not feel compelled to have an extravagant shop, use boastful advertisements, or rent the most desirable and expensive location in order to have a prosperous business. Of course, his shop should be clean and orderly, he should announce the availability of his product and be located conveniently for customers. But he must not trust in these things as the reason for his ultimate success. A believer should rest and trust only in God.

The children of God often use such expressions as "This is our busy time," or "This is our slow time." This implies that they are not seeking God daily about their calling. Instead, they ascribe their prosperity to times and seasons. The scripture, "He did not many mighty works there because of their unbelief" (Matthew 13:58) contains a truth which may be applied here. The child of God should say, "About this time of the year, business is generally slow. But I desire to serve God in my business and to help those who are in need. By prayer and faith, I can obtain a blessing from my heavenly Father, although this is usually not a busy season."

A further reason why God may not bless His children in their business may be because they are careful to hire "good salesmen"—people who have such persuasive ways that they gain an advantage over the customers. They convince them not only to buy the articles for which they ask, whether suitable or not, but they also induce customers to buy things they did not intend to buy at all. This is no less than defrauding people in a subtle way, leading them into the sin of purchasing beyond their means or, at least, spending their money needlessly. Although such sinful tricks may be allowed to prosper in the case of a man of the world, a child of God who uses such tactics will not be blessed.

Another reason why children of God do not succeed in their calling is that they try to begin their business with too little capital. If a believer has no capital at all, or very little capital in comparison with what his business requires, he should ask himself, "If it is my heavenly Father's will that I begin this business, He would have given me the money I need to get started. And since He has not, is this a plain indication that for now I should remain at my present job?"

God can provide the money in a variety of ways. But if He does not remove the hindrance, and the brother still goes into business and buys everything he needs on credit, he will only give himself reason to worry about bills. The best thing for a brother to do in this circumstance is to acknowledge his sin and seek God's merciful help to bring him into a right position.

Suppose all these previous points are carried out, but we neglect to seek God's blessing on our calling. We should not be surprised if we meet with difficulty upon difficulty. It is not enough that we seek God's help for spiritual things. We should seek His help and blessing by prayer and supplication for all our ordinary concerns in life. "Trust in the Lord with all thine heart; and lean not unto thine own understanding. In all thy ways acknowledge him, and he shall direct thy paths" (Proverbs 3:5-6).

May 30. Our work among the Orphans is growing. Since the formation of the institution in 1834 until today, 5,343 children were taught in the various day schools in Bristol alone. The Sunday school had 2,379 people and 1,896 persons were in the adult school. We also assisted thousands in the schools outside of Bristol. The Lord gladdened our hearts by the working of His Holy Spirit among the orphans.

I am depending on God alone to enlarge the orphan work. Before I told anyone else what I planned to do, I gave the record of my thoughts on this subject to a dear Christian friend to read. I did this so that I might have the counsel of a prayerful, wise, and cautious man of God. When this brother returned the manuscript, he encouraged me and gave me some money for the building fund. This was my first donation for the house, and it was a precious confirmation to me that I should go ahead with my plans.

June 21. Twenty-four days have passed since I have waited in faith on the Lord for money. So far only a little more than twenty-eight pounds have come in, but I am not discouraged. The less that comes in, the more earnestly I pray, the more I look out for answers, and the more assured I am that the Lord, in His own time, will send me all I need.

August 12. I have been praying earnestly every

day that the Lord would send in money for the building fund. My soul is at peace, although only a little money has come in. Satan tries to shake my confidence and lead me to question whether I had been mistaken concerning this whole matter. Yet he has not been allowed to triumph over me. I have asked the Lord to refresh my spirit by sending a large donation.

This morning I received five hundred pounds for the new building. I was expecting a large donation, and I would not have been surprised if five thousand pounds had come in. Praise the Lord for this precious encouragement!

September 13. Patience and faith are still needed. My desire is to let patience have its perfect work. Not one penny has come in today for the building fund, but five more orphans have applied for admission. The more I look at things according to natural appearances, the less likely it seems that I will ever get the sum I need. But I have faith in God, and my expectation is from Him alone. The Lord can change the circumstances instantly. I continue, therefore, to wait upon God and seek to encourage my heart by His Word. While He delays giving me answers, I will be occupied in His blessed work. The number of applications for admission of orphans quickens me to prayer and encourages me that the Lord will give me the desire of my heart—to provide a home for these children.

March 17, 1852. My heart has been greatly

encouraged by a donation of nearly one thousand pounds. I cannot describe to anyone how refreshing this donation is to my faith. After waiting for weeks and receiving so little, this answer to many prayers is sweet to my spirit.

May 20. Several of the orphans who left the establishment during this year had been converted before they left. Several other young people who were under our care a few years ago are strong Christians today. The spiritual growth of children gives us joy and comfort. Amid difficulties, trials, and discouragements, we have abundant reason to praise God for His goodness and to go forward in the strength of the Lord.

Chapter 23

MORE WORK AND GREATER MIRACLES

January 4, 1853. For many months I have been assured that the Lord, in His own time, would give larger sums of money for this work. At last He has answered my request. I received the promise of a donation of eight thousand one hundred pounds from a group of Christians. See how precious it is to wait on God! See how those who do so are not disappointed! Faith and patience may be tried, but in the end, those who honor God will not be put to shame.

The size of the donation did not surprise me because I expect great things from God. Have I been boasting in God in vain? Is it not obvious that it is precious to depend on God for everything? The principles I use are not only applicable to the work of God on a small scale but also in the largest operations for God.

May 26. The current expenses of the institution were never this great during the past nineteen years. But the extent of its operations and the supplies which the Lord sent in were also never so abundant.

We are richly rewarded for waiting on God. He listens to the supplications of His children who put their trust in Him. But in order to have prayers answered, a Christian must make his requests to God on the ground of the merits and worthiness of the Lord Jesus. He must not depend on his own worthiness and merits.

Do you really believe in Jesus? Do you depend on Him alone for the salvation of your soul? Make certain that not even the least degree of your own righteousness is presented to God as a ground for acceptance. If you believe in the Lord Jesus, the things you request should be for God's honor.

Suppose that we believers in the Lord Jesus make our requests to God. Suppose also that, as far as we can honestly judge, the obtaining of our requests would be for our spiritual good and for the honor of God. We must then *continue* in prayer until the blessing is given to us. Furthermore, we have to *believe* that God does hear us and will answer our prayers. Frequently we fail in not *continuing* in prayer until the blessing is obtained and in not *expecting* the blessing. As assuredly as any individual uses these points, so assuredly will his requests be granted.

October 9. This morning before breakfast I read Luke 7. While reading the account of Jesus raising the widow's son from the dead, I lifted up my heart and said, "Lord Jesus, You have the same power now. You can provide me with means for Your work. Please do so."

About half an hour later I received two hundred and thirty pounds to be used where it was needed most. The joy such answers to prayer gives me cannot be described. I was determined to wait upon God only and not to work an unscriptural deliverance for myself. I have thousands of pounds set aside for the building fund, but I would not touch it. My soul magnifies the Lord for His goodness!

The natural mind is prone to reason when we ought to believe, to be at work when we ought to be quiet, or to go our own way when we ought to steadily walk in God's ways. When I was first converted, I would have said, "What harm can there be to use some of the money which has been given for the building fund? God will help me eventually with money for the orphans, and then I can replace it." But each time we work a deliverance of our own, we find it more difficult to trust in God. At last we give way entirely to our natural reasoning, and unbelief prevails.

How different, if one waits for God's own time and looks to Him for help and deliverance! When at last help comes, after many hours of prayer and after much faith and patience, how sweet it is! What a reward the soul receives for trusting in God and waiting patiently for His deliverance! If you have never walked in this path of obedience before, do so now. You will experience the sweetness of the joy that faith brings.

December 15. I praise, adore, and magnify the Lord for His love and faithfulness in carrying me from year to year through His service and supplying me with all I need! Without His help and support, I would be completely overpowered in a very short time. With His help I go on and am very happy in my service. I am even in better health now than I was twenty years ago.

For the past several years, Bible distribution has become more important to me. The powers of darkness have attempted to rob the Church of the Holy Scriptures. Therefore, I have taken advantage of every opportunity to distribute the Bible throughout the world. Many servants of Christ in various parts of the world have helped me in this work. Through them, thousands of copies of the Bible have been distributed.

If you are in the habit of distributing tracts and have never seen fruit, I suggest the following hints for your prayerful consideration:

1. Through prayer and meditation on the Word, become willing to let God have all the glory if any good is accomplished by your service. If you desire honor for yourself, the Lord must put you aside as a vessel unfit for the Master's use. One of the greatest qualifications for usefulness in the service of the Lord is a heart that truly desires to honor Him.

2. Precede all your labors with earnest, diligent

prayer. Do not rest on the number of tracts you have given because a million tracts may not lead to the conversion of one single soul. Yet, a blessing beyond calculation may result from one single tract. Expect everything to come from the blessing of the Lord and nothing at all from your own exertions.

3. At the same time, work! Walk through every open door, be ready in season and out of season as if everything depended on your labor. This is one of the great secrets in connection with successful service for the Lord—work as if everything depended on your diligence, and trust in the blessing of the Lord to bring success.

4. This blessing of the Lord, however, should not merely be sought in prayer, but it should also be expected. The result will be that we will surely have it.

5. Suppose that, for the trial of our faith, this blessing is withheld from our sight for a long time. Or suppose we die before we see much good resulting from our labors. Our labors, if carried on in the right way, will be at last abundantly rewarded, and we will have a rich harvest in the day of Christ.

At the beginning of this period there were 300 orphans in the new Orphan House on Ashley Down. During the year 30 orphans were admitted making 330 in all. The total number of orphans who were under our care from April, 1836 to May 26, 1854 was 558.

During the past year my faith was tried in a way it had never been before. My beloved daughter, my only child and a believer for several years, became ill. The illness turned to typhus, and there seemed to be no hope for her recovery. But faith triumphed. My beloved wife and I gave her into the hands of the Lord, and He sustained us both. My soul was in perfect peace, trusting my heavenly Father. She remained very ill for more than two weeks before she began to grow stronger and was moved to Clevedon to recover.

Of all the trials of faith I have passed through, this was the greatest. By God's abundant mercy, I was able to delight myself in God, and He gave me the desire of my heart. God is always faithful to those who trust in Him.

Chapter 24

CONTINUED PROSPERITY AND GROWTH

May 26, 1855. Although I did not have all the money necessary to begin to build the new Orphan House, I began to look for land. For the past four years I never had a doubt that it was the will of God that I build accommodations for seven hundred more orphans. Yet I could see the advantages of having two houses instead of one. I checked to see whether another house could be built on each side of the present Orphan House.

After I measured the ground and found it could be done, I called in the architects to survey the area and to make a rough plan of two houses, one on each side. We would not only save money by this plan, but the direction and inspection of the whole establishment would be much easier because the buildings would be close together. We would still have plenty of land to grow our own vegetables. Once I saw what could be accomplished on the ground we owned already, I decided to build, without any further delay at the south side of the new Orphan House. The plans are now ready; and as soon as all the necessary preliminary arrangements can be made, the work will begin.

This house is intended to accommodate four hundred female orphans. With regard to the other house to be built at the north side of the new Orphan House, nothing definite can be stated at present. Enough money is available to build and furnish the house for four hundred orphans, and we expect that something will be left over. But there is not sufficient money to begin to build both.

A strong call is on my life for caring for destitute orphans. Seven hundred and fifteen orphans are now waiting for admission to this Orphan House. Only thirty-nine orphan homes provide care for three thousand seven hundred and sixty-four orphans. When the new Orphan House was being built, nearly six thousand young orphans were living in the prisons of England because there was no other place for them to go. To prevent them from going to prison and being brought up in sin, and to win their souls for God, I desire to enlarge the present establishment so that we are able to receive one thousand orphans. Individuals who have chosen not to live for the present time but for eternity will have the opportunity to help me care for these children. It is a great honor to be allowed to do anything for the Lord. When the day of recompense comes, our only regret will be that we have done so little for Him, not that we have done too much.

If anyone desires to live a life of faith and trust in God he must:

1. Not merely *say* that he trusts in God but must *really do so*. Often individuals profess to trust in God, but they embrace every opportunity where they may directly or indirectly tell someone about their need. I do not say it is wrong to make known our financial situation, but it hardly displays trust in God to expose our needs for the sake of getting other people to help us. God will take us at our word. If we do trust in Him, we must be satisfied to stand with Him alone.

2. The individual who desires to live this way must be content whether he is rich or poor. He must be willing to live in abundance or in poverty. He must be willing to leave this world without any possessions.

3. He must be willing to take the money in God's way, not merely in large sums, but in small. Many times I have had a single shilling given to me. To have refused such tokens of Christian love would have been ungracious.

4. He must be willing to live as the Lord's steward. If anyone does not give out of the blessings which the Lord gives to him, then the Lord, who influences the hearts of His children to give, would soon cause those channels to be dried up. My good income increased even more when I determined that, by God's help, His poor and His

work would be helped by my money. From that time on, the Lord was pleased to entrust me with more.

May 26, 1856. Yesterday evening it was twenty-four years since I came to labor in Bristol. In looking back on the Lord's goodness to my family and myself, the Scriptural Knowledge Institution, and the saints among whom I seek to serve Him, I exclaim, "What has God wrought!" I marvel at His kindness, and yet I do not. If I remain longer on earth, I would expect even more manifestations of His love.

The Lord continues to allow us to see fruit in connection with the orphan work. He is working in the hearts and lives of those who are now under our care. We often hear that those who were formerly under our care have become Christians and are living for the Lord. The kindness and grace of God is drawing many children to Him at the Orphan House.

November 12, 1857. The long looked-for and long prayed-for day has now arrived, and the desire of my heart was granted to me. I opened the house for four hundred more orphans today. How precious this was to me after praying every day for seven years. This blessing did not come unexpectedly to me but had been looked for and had been expected in the full assurance of faith, in God's own time.

November 20. The boiler at the new Orphan House No. 1 leaked considerably. We thought that it would last through the winter, although we suspected it was nearly worn out. For me to do nothing and say, "I will trust in God" would be careless presumption, not faith in God.

The condition of the boiler could not be known without taking down the brickwork surrounding it. What then was to be done? For the children, especially the younger infants, I was deeply concerned that they would suffer for lack of warmth. But how were we to obtain heat? The installation of a new boiler would probably take many weeks. Repairing the boiler was a questionable matter because of the size of the leak. Nothing could be decided until the brick-chamber was at least partially removed. That would take days, and what was to be done in the meantime to find warm rooms for three hundred children?

At last I decided to open the brick chamber and see the extent of the damage. The day was set when the workmen were to come, and all the necessary arrangements were made. The heat, of course, had to be shut off while the repairs were going on.

After the day was set for the repairs, a bleak north wind set in, bringing the first really cold weather of the winter. The repairs could not be put off, so I asked the Lord for two things—that He would change the north wind into a south wind, and that He would give to the workmen a desire to work. I remembered how much Nehemiah accomplished in fifty-two days while building the walls of Jerusalem because "the people had a mind to work" (Nehemiah 4:6).

The memorable day came. The evening before, the bleak north wind still blew, but on Wednesday, the south wind blew, exactly as I had prayed. The weather was so mild that no heat was needed. The brickwork was removed, the leak was soon found, and the repairmen set to work.

About half-past eight in the evening, when I was going to leave for my home, I was informed that the manager of the repair firm had arrived to see how the work was going on. I went to the cellar to see him and the men. The manager said, "The men will work late this evening and come very early again tomorrow."

"We would rather, sir," said the foreman, "work all night."

Then I remembered the second part of my prayer—that God would give the men "a mind to work." By the next morning, the repair of the boiler was accomplished. Within thirty hours the brickwork was up again, and the fire was in the boiler. All the time, the south wind blew so mildly that there was not the least need for any heat.

Chapter 25

THE SPIRIT'S WORK AMONG US

February 2, 1858. I took the first steps toward building the third house. A lady in London, a complete stranger to me, ordered her bankers to send three hundred pounds for the support of the orphans. I was also informed that in two weeks eight hundred pounds will be paid to me for the work of the Lord.

The three hundred pounds was sent the next day, and the eight hundred pounds arrived two weeks later. As the work grows, the Lord keeps pace with the expenses, helping when help is really needed, often even giving beforehand.

During the year 1857-1858, twenty-four schools were supported or assisted out of the funds of the institution, nearly four thousand Bibles and portions of Scripture were distributed, and over three thousand five hundred pounds were expended for the aid of eighty-two missionaries. I was later told that the money often came when the missionaries did not have a shilling left.

More than one million tracts and books were also distributed. Letters received from the people who distributed them show that they were greatly used in awakening and converting souls.

During the past twenty-two years, the Spirit of God has been working among the orphans; and many of them have come to know the Lord. But we never had so great a work take place as during the past year.

On May 26, 1857, Caroline Bailey, one of the orphans, died. The death of this beloved girl, who had known the Lord for several months, was used by the Lord to answer our daily prayers for the conversion of the orphans. All at once, more than fifty of the girls began to ask questions about heaven, hell, and eternity.

Young people often get concerned about the things of God, but these impressions pass away before long. I have seen this myself, having dealt with many thousands of children and teenagers during the last thirty years. If this spiritual awakening among the orphans had begun within the last few days, or even weeks, I would not have mentioned it. But more than a year has elasped, and in addition to those ten who were previously believers, twenty-three more girls have accepted Jesus as their Savior. In addition to this, some of the other girls in the new Orphan House No. 2 and some of the boys also are interested in the things of God. Our labors have already begun to be blessed to the hearts of some of the newly-admitted orphans.

February 17, 1858. As far as I am able to judge, I now have all the financial means I require for the third house also. I am able to accomplish the full enlargement of the orphan work to one thousand orphans.

October 29. In the last report I stated that I was looking for land for the third house. I waited daily on God, and He has exercised my faith and patience. More than once when I seemed to have obtained my desire, I again appeared further from it than ever. Being fully assured that the Lord's time had not yet come, I continued to pray and to exercise faith. I knew He would finally help.

Last month I obtained eleven and a half acres of land with a house which is close to the new Orphan Houses and only separated from them by the road. The price for house and land was more money than I wanted to spend on the site, but it was important that the third house be near the other two to facilitate the superintendence and direction. The longer I go on in this service, the more I find that prayer and faith can overcome every difficulty.

Now that I have the land, I want to make the best use of it and build for four hundred orphans, instead of for three hundred as I had previously planned. After several meetings with the architects, I learned that it was possible to accommodate, with comparatively little more expense, four hundred and fifty orphans. I finally decided on that number. This means that I will eventually have one thousand one hundred and fifty orphans under my care.

January 4, 1859. I received seven thousand pounds left entirely at my disposal for the work of God. When I decided to build for four hundred and fifty orphans, instead of three hundred, I needed several thousand pounds more. I was fully assured that God would give me the money because I made the decision in reliance on Him and for the honor of His name. The Lord has honored my faith in Him!

May 26. During the past year, we have not seen as great and sudden a work of the Spirit of God among the orphans as during the previous years. Yet, the blessing of the Lord has continued. Many are showing an interest in the things of God among the four hundred and twenty-four orphans who were admitted within the last eighteen months. They have asked to be allowed to take their Bibles with them to bed so that, if they awake in the morning before the bell is rung, they may be able to read.

When I began the orphan work, one of my goals was to benefit the Church by my written accounts of this service. I confidently anticipated that my answers to prayer would lead believers to look for answers to their own prayers and encourage them to bring all their needs before God. I also firmly believed that many unconverted persons would see that there is reality in the things of God.

As I expected, so it has been. The reports of this institution have been used by God to convert many people. In thousands of instances, believers have been benefited through them, being comforted, encouraged, led to simply believe the Word of God, and to trust in Him for everything.

December 9. Today it is twenty-four years since the orphan work began. What a marvelous miracle God has done! We now have 700 orphans under our care.

December 10. The following letter was received today from an apprentice—

Most Beloved Sir:

With feelings of gratitude and great thankfulness to you for all the kindness I received while under your care, and for now apprenticing me to a suitable trade to earn my own living, I write you these few lines. I arrived at my destination safely and was kindly received by my employer. Dear sir, I thank you for the education, food, clothing, and for every comfort. But, above all, I thank you for the instruction from God's Word I received in that Orphan House. There I was brought to know Jesus as my Savior. I hope to have Him as my guide through all my difficulties, temptations, and trials in this world. With Him for my guide, I hope to prosper in my trade, and thereby show my gratitude to you for all the kindness I have received.

Please accept my gratitude and thanks. I hope you will have many, many more years to care for children like me. I am sure I will often look back with pleasure and regret to the time I was in that happy home—with pleasure that I lived there, and with regret that I left it. Please accept my grateful thanks and give my love to my teachers.

Day after day, and year after year, we pray for the spiritual benefit of the orphans under our care. These supplications have been abundantly answered by the conversion of hundreds of the orphans. We are encouraged to wait on God for even greater blessings.

March 1, 1860. A great work of the Spirit of God began in January and February among the six-to-nine year old girls. It extended to the older girls and then to the boys. Within ten days nearly 200 of the orphans found peace through faith in our Lord Jesus. They asked to be allowed to hold prayer meetings among themselves, and they have had these meetings ever since. Many of them expressed their concern about the salvation of their friends and relatives, and they spoke or wrote to them about how to be saved.

During no year have we had greater cause for thanksgiving on account of the spiritual blessing among the children than during the last—and we look for even further and greater blessings.

CONCLUSION

What God has done for Mr. Muller and his associates, we cannot doubt that, under the same conditions, He will do for every believing disciple of Christ. Not only did Mr. Muller trust in God that all the financial means he needed would be furnished, but that, in answer to prayer, wisdom would be given him to manage the work. The result surpassed his highest expectations. If anyone will undertake any Christian work in a similar spirit and on the same principles, his labor will meet with a similar result.

Immediate results will not always be seen, however. We must not try to limit the omniscience of God by the short-sighted ignorance of man. It may best suit the purpose of infinite goodness to delay an answer to the prayer of faith. Crosses and disappointments may be experienced while we wait on God. But in the end these will promote the object to be accomplished.

There is no reason why we should not take the

case of Mr. Muller as an example for our imitation. Whoever has this same simple desire in all things to do the will of God and the same childlike trust in His promises may hope for a similar blessing. God is no respecter of persons. "If any man doeth his will, him he heareth" (John 9:31).

All the teaching of the Scriptures confirm this belief. In the Scriptures, every form of illustration is used to show us that God is indeed our Father and that He delights to grant our requests for anything that is for our benefit and His glory. He pledges Himself to direct and help everyone who honestly labors to promote real faith in His Word.

No Christian, however poor and humble, should despair of doing a noble work for God. He never needs to wait until he can obtain the cooperation of the multitude or the wealthy. Let him undertake what he believes to be his duty, on ever so small a scale, and look directly to God for aid and direction. If God has planted the seed, it will take root, grow, and bear fruit. "It is better to trust in the Lord than to put confidence in man. It is better to trust the Lord than to put confidence in princes" (Psalm 118:8-9).

George Muller was a living demonstration of the reality of the Scripture, "But my God shall supply all your need according to his riches in glory by Christ Jesus" (Philippians 4:19).

H. Lincoln Wayland

Prayer and Faith
R. A. Torrey

Put prayer (a petition to God) and faith (belief and trust in God) together, and the result is incredible power! Whether you are a new believer or have been a Christian for decades, the recipe for spiritual success is within your reach. R. A. Torrey reveals how you can prevail in prayer, be effective in soulwinning, and come to an intimate understanding of God and His Word. Discover how the ingredients of prayer and faith will produce a life of spiritual power and strength for you.

ISBN: 0-88368-759-3 • Trade • 576 pages

www.whitakerhouse.com

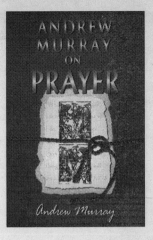

Andrew Murray on Prayer
Andrew Murray

Combining seven of Andrew Murray's most treasured works on prayer, this book will give you biblical guidelines for effective communication with God. Discover essential keys to developing a vital prayer life, including how to receive clear direction from the Lord, see your unsaved loved ones come to Christ, and overcome temptation. Lovingly explained, the principles presented here will permanently transform your prayer life!

ISBN: 0-88368-528-0 • Trade • 656 pages

www.whitakerhouse.com

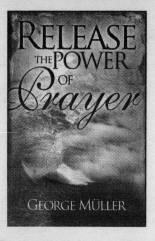

Release the Power of Prayer
George Müller

As a boy, George Müller was a thief and a liar, but after turning to Christ, he provided for over 10,000 orphans—without ever asking anyone but God to supply their needs. He testified that he knew of at least 50,000 specific answers to his prayers. From his amazing personal account, you will find out how to watch God turn impossibilities into reality. Discover how to trust God and seek His answers to your every problem, and experience the same miraculous hand of God at work in your life today.

ISBN: 0-88368-795-X • Trade • 144 pages